Visual Reference

Microsoft
Outlook 2000
At a Glance

G000137844

Microsoft Press

PUBLISHED BY
Microsoft Press
A Division of Microsoft Corporation
One Microsoft Way
Redmond, Washington 98052-6399

Copyright © 1999 by Stephen L. Nelson, Inc.

Library of Congress Cataloging-in-Publication Data
Nelson, Stephen L., 1959-
    Microsoft Outlook 2000 At a Glance / Stephen L. Nelson.
      p. cm.
   Includes index.
   ISBN 1-57231-948-8
    1. Microsoft Outlook.   2. Time management--Computer programs.
   3. Personal information management--Computer programs. I. Title.
   II. Title: Microsoft Outlook Two Thousand At a Glance.
   HD69.T54N454   1999
   005.369--dc21   98-43579
                                                               CIP

Printed and bound in the United States of America.

1 2 3 4 5 6 7 8 9 QEQE   4 3 2 1 0 9

Distributed in Canada by ITP Nelson, a division of Thomson Canada Limited.

A CIP catalogue record for this book is available from the British Library.

Microsoft Press books are available through booksellers and distributors worldwide. For further information about international editions, contact your local Microsoft Corporation office or contact Microsoft Press International directly at fax (425) 936-7329. Visit our Web site at mspress.microsoft.com.

For Stephen L. Nelson, Inc.
Writers: Jason Gerend and Steve Nelson
Project Editor: Paula Thurman
Technical Editor: Brian Milbrath

For Microsoft Press
Acquisitions Editor: Susanne M. Forderer
Project Editor: Laura Sackerman

Contents

See today's tasks, appointments, and e-mail notifications all in one place.
See page 8

"How do I attach a file to an e-mail message?"

See page 40

"How do I add a contact to my Contacts folder?"

See page 54

Todd Young

Search your Address Book for a contact's e-mail address. See page 74

Print a daily or
weekly calendar.
See page 101

*"How do I
delegate a task to
someone?"*

See page 119

"How do I save an Outlook folder to a disk or network drive?"

See page 150

Organize your Inbox with folders and colors.
See pages 160–161

Using Colors

"How do I automatically empty the Deleted Items folder?"

See page 180

Add a signature to all of your outgoing messages.
See page 185

About This Book

*M*icrosoft Outlook 2000 At a Glance is for anyone who wants to exploit the power of Microsoft's personal information manager and electronic mail client, Outlook 2000. I think you'll find this book to be a straightforward, easy-to-read, and easy-to-use reference tool. Based on the premise that personal information managers and electronic mail are tools that everyone can use, this book's purpose is to help you use your computer as a tool to work smarter (not just harder) and to better plan and organize your life (especially your work).

No Computerese!

Let's face it—when there's a task you don't know how to do but you need to get it done in a hurry, or when you're stuck in the middle of a task and can't figure out what to do next, there's nothing more frustrating than having to read page after page of technical background material. You want the information you need—nothing more, nothing less— and you want it now! And the information should be easy to find and understand.

That's what this book is all about. It's written in plain English—no technical jargon and no computerese. No single task in the book takes more than two pages. Just look up the task in the index or the table of contents, turn to the page, and there it is. Each task introduction gives you information that is essential to performing the task, suggesting situations in which you can use the task or providing examples of the benefit you gain from completing the procedure. The task itself is laid out step by step and accompanied by a graphics image that adds visual clarity. Just read the introduction, follow the steps, look at the illustrations, and get your work done with a minimum of hassle.

You may want to turn to another task if the one you're working on has a "See Also" in the left column. Because there's a lot of overlap among tasks, I didn't want to keep repeating myself; you might find more elementary or more advanced tasks laid out on the pages referenced. I've also added some useful tips here and there and offered a "Try This" once in a while to give you a context in which to use the task. But by and large, I've tried to remain true to the heart and soul of the book, which is that the information you need should be available to you *at a glance*.

What's New

If you're looking for what's new in Outlook 2000, just look for this new icon **New**2000 inserted throughout the book. You will find the new icon in the table of contents so you can quickly and easily identify new or improved features in Outlook. You will also find the new icon on the first page of each section. There it will serve as a handy reminder of the latest improvements in Outlook as you move from one task to another.

Useful Tasks...

Whether you use Outlook 2000 as a full-blown personal information manager or simply as a way to send and receive electronic mail, I've tried to pack this book with procedures for everything I could think of that you might want to do, from the simplest tasks to some of the more esoteric ones.

...And the Easiest Way to Do Them

Another thing I've tried to do in *Microsoft Outlook* 2000 *At a Glance* is to find and document the easiest way to accomplish a task. Outlook 2000 often provides many ways to obtain a single result, which can be daunting or delightful, depending on the way you like to work. If you tend to stick with one favorite and familiar approach, the methods described in this book are the way to go. If you prefer to try out alternative techniques, go ahead! The intuitiveness of Outlook invites exploration, and you're likely to discover ways of doing things that you think are easier or that you like better. If you do, that's great! It's exactly what the creators of Outlook had in mind when they provided so many alternatives.

A Quick Overview

You don't have to read this book in any particular order. The book is designed so that you can jump in, get the information you need, and then close the book, keeping it near your computer until the next time you need it. But that doesn't mean I scattered the information about with wild abandon. If you were to read the book from front to back, you'd find a logical progression from the simple tasks to the more complex ones. Here's a quick overview.

Section 2 introduces Outlook, explains how you can integrate Outlook into your work, and describes some Outlook basics that you'll want to know as you begin exploring this useful tool.

If you're connected to the Internet or a local area network, you'll want to review Sections 3, 4, and 5. Section 3 describes how you use Outlook for sending and receiving electronic mail, or e-mail. Section 4 describes how you can keep an electronic Contacts list and log using Outlook, as well as get maps and directions to your contacts. Section 5 shows how you can create an electronic Address Book, which you can use for, among other things, corresponding by e-mail. And Section 6 introduces another way you can correspond electronically: using Microsoft Outlook Express to read and post messages to electronic newsgroups.

Sections 7, 8, 9, and 10 describe how Outlook's personal information management tools work. Section 7 explains Outlook's appointment Calendar. Section 8 shows how you use Outlook's Tasks list to plan your work and prioritize your tasks. Section 9 describes how Outlook's Journal lets you integrate different types of information to record your daily activities. Finally, Section 10 explains how you can use Outlook's Notes to jot down reminders to yourself.

The remaining two sections of this book delve into more advanced topics: Section 11, for example, explains how you can use Outlook as a desktop manager. (Once you begin using Outlook to organize your work and life, why not also use it as a tool for organizing your computer's resources?) Section 12 explains how you can customize the way Outlook looks and works.

A Final Word (or Two)

Outlook comes with the web browser Microsoft Internet Explorer 5 and the newsreader Outlook Express. This book focuses on Outlook 2000 and Outlook Express. Section 7 also briefly introduces Microsoft NetMeeting, an Internet Explorer add-on component. For more information on Internet Explorer 5 and its other components, check out a copy of *Internet Explorer 5 At a Glance* published by Microsoft Press.

I had three goals in writing this book. I want this book to help you:

◆ Do all the things you want to do with Outlook 2000.
◆ Discover how to do things you didn't know you wanted to do with Outlook.
◆ Enjoy using Outlook.

My "thank you" for buying this book is the achievement of those goals. I hope you'll have as much fun using *Microsoft Outlook 2000 At a Glance* as I've had writing it. The best way to learn is by doing, and that's what I hope you'll get from this book.

Jump right in!

2

Introducing Outlook

Microsoft Outlook is easy to use. And that's especially true if you've worked with other Microsoft Office applications such as Microsoft Word or Microsoft Excel. Nevertheless, you'll find it helpful to acquaint yourself with Outlook's basic organization and with the information it manages before venturing more deeply into its functionality.

Specifically, you'll want to understand two key concepts. First you'll need to know that Outlook collects and processes a variety of information: e-mail messages, appointments, contacts (name and address information), tasks, and notes. In the language of Outlook, these pieces of information are all called items. An e-mail message, for example, is an item. So is an appointment entered in Outlook's appointment Calendar. And so is a task you've recorded in Outlook's Tasks list.

The second bit of information that you'll want to understand is that Outlook uses folders to organize its items by type. E-mail messages, for example, are stored in Mail folders. Appointments are stored in the Calendar folder, tasks are stored in the Tasks folder, and contacts (name and address information) are stored in still another folder, called the Contacts folder.

Running the Outlook Startup Wizard

You can install Outlook in a variety of different ways, depending on whether and how you want to use Outlook to send and receive e-mail, and whether you have used a previous e-mail client that you want to upgrade. You can use Outlook with a wide variety of messaging and information sources, including Internet service providers (ISPs), Microsoft Fax, and an Exchange server. Or you can choose to set up Outlook for no e-mail usage, and instead use only its task, contact, and schedule management features.

> **TIP**
>
> **Set the default for News and Contacts.** *Outlook may tell you that it currently isn't the default manager for News and Contacts after installation. Click Yes if you want to use Outlook to manage your newsgroups and contacts. Click No to continue using your current program.*

Run the Outlook Startup Wizard

1. Install Outlook 2000 (if not already installed) from your Outlook 2000 CD or another package that includes Outlook, such as Microsoft Office 2000.

2. Double-click the Outlook icon on your desktop to start Outlook. The first time you start Outlook, the Outlook Startup Wizard begins.

3. Click Next to begin setting up Outlook. Outlook setup may proceed differently than described here, depending on the e-mail services you currently use.

4. If you have an earlier version of Outlook installed on your computer and you want to use your current Outlook settings, click Yes and then click Next to immediately open Outlook with your current settings. Otherwise, click No, and then click Next.

5. If you want to import e-mail settings, messages, and address books from an e-mail client other than Outlook, select the client and click Next to complete the Startup Wizard. Otherwise, select None Of The Above, and click Next.

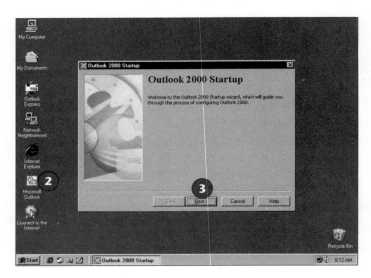

TIP

Internet Only installation.
To use features such as IMAP mail folders and scheduling over the Internet, you need to install the Internet Only version. If you install this version, your screens may appear slightly different from the screens pictured in this book.

TIP

Use the My Documents folder. *Backing up your files is easier if you put your Outlook files in the My Documents folder. To do this, click the Change Folder button and then browse to your My Documents folder or a folder inside it.*

TIP

Change e-mail options.
You can change your e-mail service options as your needs change. To switch to a different option after installing Outlook, choose Options from the Tools menu, click the Mail Delivery tab, and then click Reconfigure Mail Support.

6 Choose the type of e-mail service you plan on using with Outlook, and click Next.

- ◆ Click the Internet Only option button if you only use an Internet service provider to send and receive Internet mail.
- ◆ Click the Corporate Or Workgroup option button if you want to send and receive mail over a network.
- ◆ Click the No E-Mail option button if you do not want to use Outlook for sending and receiving e-mail.

2

Working with Outlook Today

With Outlook Today, you can view the day's happenings at a glance—you can see what tasks you have to do, whether you have new e-mail, and what events are coming up. Using Outlook Today, you can go to different parts of Outlook with the click of a button.

TIP

Display Outlook Today when Outlook starts. *To display Outlook Today every time you start Outlook, click Customize Outlook Today. Then select the When Starting, Go Directly To Outlook Today check box. Click Save Changes to return to Outlook Today.*

TIP

Go to Outlook Today. *You can also display Outlook Today by choosing Go To from the View menu and then choosing Outlook Today.*

Display Outlook Today

1. Click the Outlook Today icon on the Outlook Bar.

2. Click a hyperlink to display your Calendar, your Messages Inbox, or your Tasks list.

The Parts of the Outlook Window

If you can't find a command, click the arrows at the bottom of a menu.

You can create any new Outlook item by clicking this down arrow and selecting the item from the list.

This is the Outlook Bar. You can move to the different Outlook folders by clicking the icons on the bar.

The Folder Banner displays the name of the folder that is currently open.

This is a group. Click here to display a different set of folder icons.

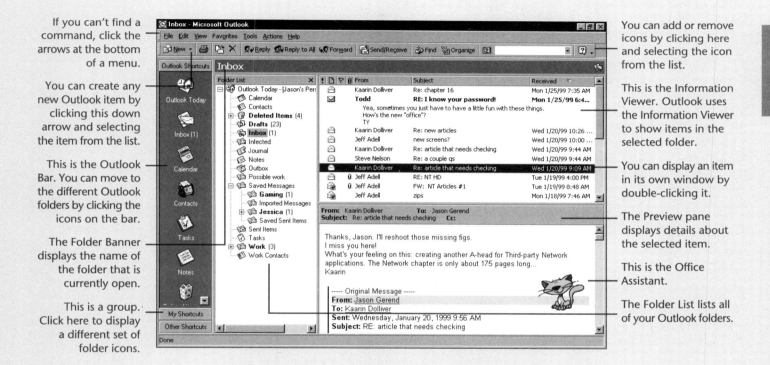

You can add or remove icons by clicking here and selecting the icon from the list.

This is the Information Viewer. Outlook uses the Information Viewer to show items in the selected folder.

You can display an item in its own window by double-clicking it.

The Preview pane displays details about the selected item.

This is the Office Assistant.

The Folder List lists all of your Outlook folders.

Getting Help

Like the other Microsoft Office applications, Outlook supplies a Help menu and an Office Assistant that you can use to get online help. Choosing Microsoft Outlook Help from the Help menu lets you use the Office Assistant or the Outlook Help file to find the information you need. The Office Assistant is a tool to help you find answers to questions that come up as you work with Outlook.

> **TIP**
>
> **Display hidden menu commands.** *Click the arrows at the bottom of a menu to display all menu commands.*

> **TIP**
>
> **Turn off the Office Assistant.** *To turn off the Office Assistant once and for all, right-click the Office Assistant and choose Options from the shortcut menu. Then clear the Use The Office Assistant check box.*

Open Microsoft Outlook Help

1 Choose Microsoft Outlook Help from the Help menu. If you turned off the Office Assistant, Microsoft Office Help will appear.

2 Click a tab to search through the help information in a different way.

- ◆ Click the Contents tab to view the contents of the Help file. Double-click a book icon to display a list of topics on a specific subject. Click a topic to display the help information.

- ◆ Click the Index tab to view an alphabetical listing of terms and functions associated with Outlook. Double-click a word or phrase to display the help information on that topic.

- ◆ Click the Answer Wizard tab to ask a question.

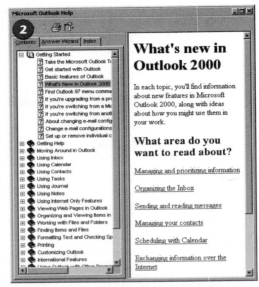

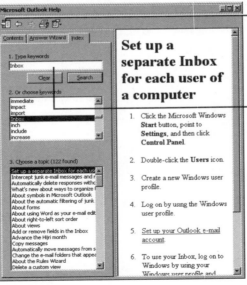

Click here to hide the Help tabs and display only the help information you requested.

Type a few letters in this text box to display a list of help topics that begin with those letters.

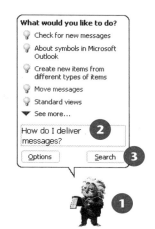

TIP

Use What's This? *If you have a question about a part of the Outlook window or what a button or box does, choose What's This? from the Help menu. Then click the object you have a question about.*

TIP

Start or hide the Office Assistant. *Choose Show The Office Assistant from the Help menu to display the Office Assistant, or choose Hide The Office Assistant to close the Office Assistant.*

Ask a Question

1. Click the Office Assistant.

2. Click the question text box, and type your question.

3. Click Search.

4. Click the button next to the topic that you want more information about.

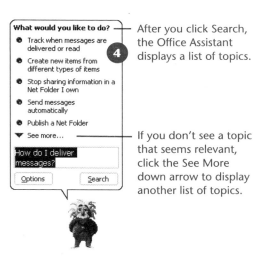

After you click Search, the Office Assistant displays a list of topics.

If you don't see a topic that seems relevant, click the See More down arrow to display another list of topics.

Using the Outlook Bar

Outlook provides many tools you can use for managing your day, your work, and your electronic correspondence. To begin using these tools, however, you'll need to learn how to work with the Outlook Bar. In essence, you click the icons on the Outlook Bar to tell Outlook what it is that you want to do.

TRY THIS

Need more room? *Right-click the background of the Outlook Bar and choose Small Icons from the shortcut menu to fit more icons on the Outlook Bar.*

TIP

Outlook 97 upgraders. *If you upgraded from Outlook 97, your Outlook Bar buttons may still be called Outlook, Mail, and Other.*

View Your Outlook Folder

1 Click the Outlook Shortcuts group.

2 Click the icon for the folder that contains the items you want to see.

◆ Click Outlook Today to see an overview of your day in Outlook.

◆ Click the Inbox icon to see messages you've received.

◆ Click the Calendar icon to display your appointment calendar. You can move to a different date by clicking the date in the Date Navigator calendar.

◆ Click the Contacts icon to view your contacts. Click the alphabet buttons to move to the contacts whose last names begin with the letters you click.

◆ Click the Tasks icon to see your task list.

◆ Click the Notes icon to create and work with Outlook's computer equivalent of sticky notes.

◆ Click the Deleted Items icon to view the items you've deleted from other Outlook folders.

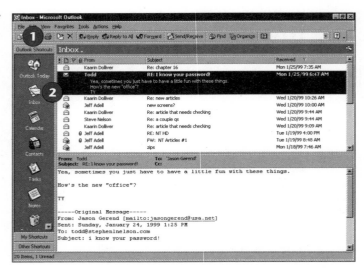

TRY THIS

Use My Computer. *To use the My Computer program, or to view the contents of your My Documents or Favorites folder on your computer, click the Other Shortcuts button.*

SEE ALSO

See Section 11, "Using Outlook as a Desktop Manager," for more information about using Outlook as an information manager.

TRY THIS

Another way of getting around. *You can use the Folder list in addition to the Outlook Bar to view and access you Outlook folders. To display the Folder list, choose Folder List from the View menu. Then select a folder from the list to display the items in that folder. You can also display the Folder list by clicking the name of the open folder on the Folder Banner. To stop displaying the Folder list, click its Close button.*

View Your Other Mail Folders

1. Click the My Shortcuts button.

2. Click the Mail folder that contains the messages you want to see.

   ◆ Click the Drafts icon to see messages you've begun but not yet sent.

   ◆ Click the Outbox icon to see messages that you have sent but that are waiting to be delivered the next time you connect to the Internet or to your network.

   ◆ Click the Sent Items icon to see messages you've already delivered.

   ◆ Click the Journal icon to see your journal entries on a timeline.

   ◆ Click the Outlook Updates icon to look for Outlook program updates on the Microsoft Office Update web site.

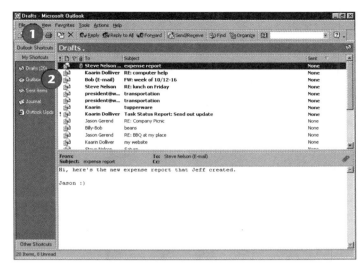

Viewing Items

Once you understand how Outlook uses folders to organize the items you create with Outlook, and once you know how to access these folders using the Outlook Bar, you'll find it useful to know more about the different ways you can view the items in these folders.

TIP

Outlook remembers Preview pane settings. *When you tell Outlook to display the Preview pane in a particular folder, Outlook continues to display the Preview pane whenever you open that folder. To stop displaying the Preview pane in a folder, open the folder and choose Preview Pane from the View menu.*

Display an Item in the Preview Pane

1 Open the folder with the item you want to display.

2 Choose Preview Pane from the View menu.

3 To display an item in the Preview pane, select the item from the item list.

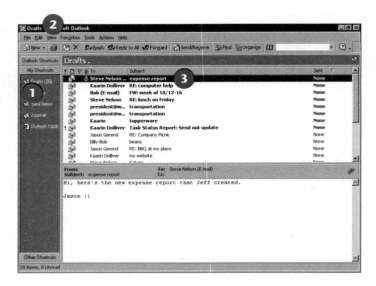

Different windows. *Outlook uses different-looking windows to display other types of items.*

Display an Item in Its Own Window

1 Open the folder with the item you want to display.

2 Double-click the item in the item list.

3 Click the Close button after you finish reviewing the item details.

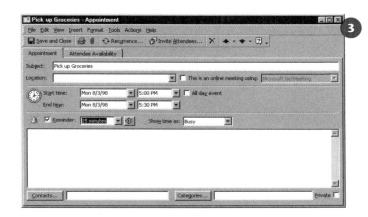

Reverse sort. *Click a column heading once to sort text items in alphabetical order. Click a column heading a second time to re-sort text items in reverse alphabetical order. Clicking the column heading for a column of dates sorts the dates in chronological or reverse chronological order.*

Sort the Items in a Folder

1 Display the folder that contains the items you want to sort.

2 Click one of the column headings in the Informa-tion Viewer to sort the items in ascending or descending order.

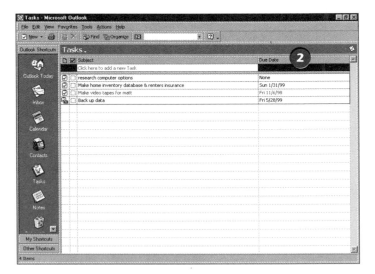

Printing Item Lists

You can print a list of the items in the Calendar, Contacts, and Tasks folders. The procedure is the same for all folders: display the folder containing the item list you want to print, and then choose Print from the File menu.

TRY THIS

Quick printing. *If you want to accept all of the default, or suggested, print settings in the Print dialog box, click the Print toolbar button instead of choosing Print from the File menu. If you do this, Outlook prints the item list without first displaying the Print dialog box.*

TRY THIS

Print preview. *To see how your printed list will look, click Preview in the Print dialog box.*

Print an Item List

1. Display the folder containing the item list you want to print.

2. Choose Print from the File menu.

3. Optionally, select the printer you want to use from the Name drop-down list box.

4. Describe how you want Outlook to print the item list by using the Print Style box and buttons.

5. Specify how many copies you want in the Number Of Copies box.

6. Click OK.

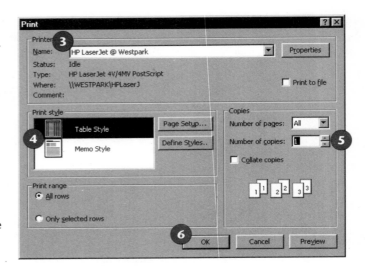

Creating New Folders

You can expand your use of the Outlook folders to better organize your Outlook items. For example, you can add folders and then use these new folders to categorize items such as e-mail messages more specifically.

TIP

Add a shortcut. *If the folder you are creating is one that you will want to access frequently, make sure you click Yes in the Add Shortcut To Outlook Bar message window that Outlook displays after you create the folder.*

TIP

Create extra folders. *If you need to manage and store a large volume of e-mail messages, you can and should create additional message folders.*

Create a New Folder

1. Choose New from the File menu.

2. Choose Folder from the New submenu.

3. Type a name for the new folder in the Name text box.

4. Specify what type of Outlook items this folder will store in the Folder Contains drop-down list box.

5. Click the folder in which you want the new folder to be a subfolder.

6. Click OK.

Moving Items Between Folders

You probably don't want your folders cluttered with hundreds of items. Instead, you want to move items that belong together into their own folders.

TIP

Use AutoCreate. *If you move an item to a different type of folder, Outlook converts the item from one type to another type. For instance, if you move a task from your Tasks folder to your Notes folder, Outlook creates a new note using the old task item's information.*

TRY THIS

Drag it. *You can also copy an item to another folder by dragging the item to the folder's icon on the Outlook Bar.*

TIP

Move open items. *If you have an item open in its own window, you can choose Move To Folder or Copy To Folder from the File menu to move or copy the item to another folder.*

Move an Item

1. Display the folder containing the item you want to move.

2. Right-click the item.

3. Choose Move To Folder from the shortcut menu.

4. Select the folder to which you want to move the item.

5. Click OK.

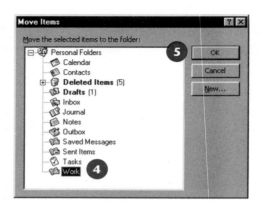

Finding Lost Items

As you accumulate items and move items to new folders to accommodate additional items, it's easy to misplace an item or two along the way. Luckily, Outlook's Advanced Find tool can help you locate lost items.

Find an Item

1 Choose Advanced Find from the Tools menu.

2 Indicate what kind of item you want to search for in the Look For drop-down list box.

3 Click Browse, and use the Select Folder(s) dialog box to select the folders you want to search.

4 Describe the item by entering text in the text boxes.

5 Specify in what part of the item Outlook should look for your search word.

6 Click Find Now.

7 If Outlook finds items that match your criteria, it lists them at the bottom of the Find window. Double-click an item to open it.

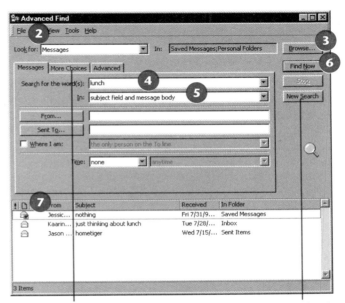

Use the More Choices tab to search for items by other characteristics, such as category or size.

Click New Search to begin a search that uses new search criteria.

Cleaning Folders

Not surprisingly, it's easy for folders to become cluttered with old or unnecessary items. So you'll want to learn the basics of keeping folders clean: how to remove items from folders, how to empty the Deleted Items folder, and, when necessary, how to undelete items you accidentally deleted.

TIP

Use the Deleted Items folder. *When you delete an item from a folder, Outlook moves the item to the Deleted Items folder. When you delete an item from the Deleted Items folder, or when the Deleted Items folder is emptied, Outlook permanently deletes the item.*

Delete an Item from a Folder

1 Display the item's folder.

2 Display the item to verify that you want to remove the item.

3 Click the Delete toolbar button.

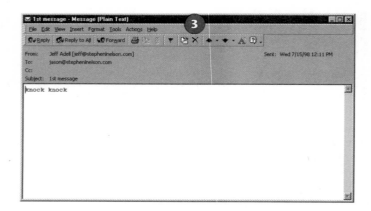

Undelete an Item

1 Display the Deleted Items folder.

2 Right-click the item you want to undelete.

3 Choose Move To Folder from the shortcut menu.

4 Select the folder from which you originally removed the item.

5 Click OK.

The Deleted Items folder vs. the Recycle Bin.
Although Outlook's Deleted Items folder uses the same icon image as the Windows Recycle Bin, it's not actually the same folder. For example, you don't empty the Recycle Bin by emptying the Deleted Items folder. You also cannot restore items you delete from the Deleted Items folder by using the Recycle Bin.

Automatically empty the Deleted Items folder. *To set up Outlook so that it empties the Deleted Items folder every time you exit Outlook, choose Options from the Tools menu and click the Other tab. Then select the Empty The Deleted Items Folder Upon Exiting check box, and click OK.*

Empty the Deleted Items Folder

1 Right-click the Deleted Items icon on the Outlook Bar.

2 Choose Empty "Deleted Items" Folder from the shortcut menu.

3 When Outlook asks, confirm that you want to delete everything in the folder by clicking Yes.

2

Working with Messages

Microsoft Outlook's most useful feature might be its ability to send and receive electronic mail (e-mail) and faxes. Using Outlook, you'll find it easy to send and receive e-mail messages over the Internet via your Internet service provider or online service. You can also send and receive faxes. If your desktop or laptop computer connects to a local area network and that network includes a Microsoft Exchange mail server, you'll also be able to use Outlook to send and receive e-mail messages over your local area network.

With Outlook—and many other e-mail clients—you aren't limited to e-mailing just textual messages. Outlook also allows you to send and receive files as well as richly formatted messages and pictures. This means that another user on your local area network with an Exchange server can send you a Microsoft Excel workbook describing next year's budget, for example, and then you can later send it back. In addition, somebody halfway around the world can send you a file—and you can send it back via your Internet service provider or online service.

Outlook's e-mail ability goes beyond that of a simple e-mail client that you can use to send and receive messages, however. Outlook provides numerous tools that make it easy to organize, store, and share fax and e-mail messages.

Receiving Messages

Whether your e-mail messages come to you from an Exchange server on a local area network or from an Internet service provider, Outlook makes it easy to receive incoming e-mail messages.

View Your Inbox

 Click the Inbox icon on the Outlook Bar to see your incoming messages.

Messages you haven't read appear in boldface.

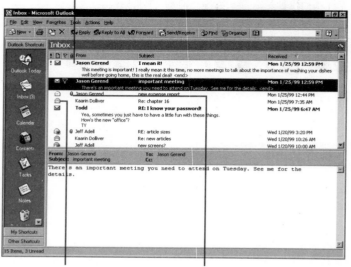

Messages you've read have an open envelope icon beside them.

Messages with attachments have a paper-clip icon beside them.

Automatic delivery. *To tell Outlook to automatically deliver messages you send, choose Options from the Tools menu, click the Mail Delivery tab, and then select the Send Messages Immediately When Connected check box. Messages you send across an Exchange Server are always delivered immediately.*

The Send And Receive button. *If you have only one e-mail message service, or if you have accounts with several services and want to check all of them for new mail, click the Send And Receive toolbar button to collect your messages.*

View received faxes. *Newly received faxes will also appear in the Inbox. Double-click a fax to open it.*

Collect Your New Messages

1 Choose Send And Receive from the Tools menu.

2 Choose the e-mail service you want to check from the submenu.

3 If you indicate that you want to collect e-mail messages from an Internet service provider, Outlook may prompt you to complete whatever sign-on procedures are required to connect to the provider.

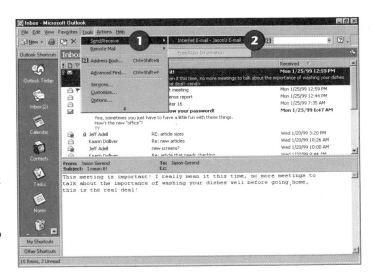

Using Remote Mail

Remote Mail is a useful feature that allows you to check your e-mail from multiple locations. With Remote Mail, if you check your e-mail at home and find some business messages, you can leave them on the server and retrieve them the next time you go to your workplace.

TIP

Disconnect. *To disconnect, choose Remote Mail from the Tools menu and then choose Disconnect, or click the Remote toolbar's Disconnect button.*

Make a Remote Mail Connection

1. Choose Remote Mail from the Tools menu, and then choose Connect.

2. Select the e-mail account or accounts you would like to connect to, and then click Next.

3. If you want to download only message headers, select the check box and then click Finish.

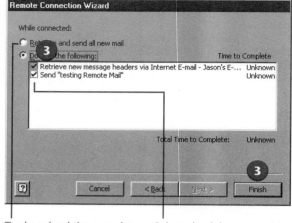

To download the complete text of all new messages, click here.

Select check boxes next to the actions you want to perform.

Work with Messages

1. Right-click a message, and choose Mark To Retrieve or Mark To Retrieve A Copy to download the full message text.

2. If you want to delete a message, select the message and click the Delete toolbar button.

3. To unmark a message you marked for download, right-click it and choose Unmark.

4. Follow the steps above to connect and process your messages.

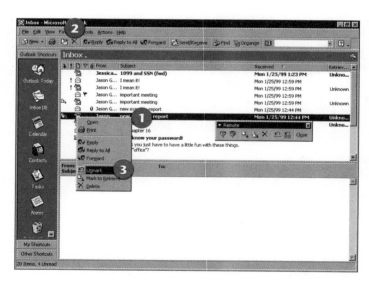

Displaying Messages

After you collect your e-mail messages in your Inbox folder, you're ready to begin reading them. To do this, you simply display the messages.

SEE ALSO

See "Replying to Messages" on page 29 for information on replying to a message and "Forwarding Messages" on page 30 for information on forwarding a message.

SEE ALSO

See "Viewing Items" on page 14 for information on displaying the Preview pane.

TIP

Close a message. *To close a Message window, click the Message window's Close button.*

Display a Message

1. Click the Inbox icon on the Outlook Bar to see your incoming messages.

2. If you have the Preview pane displayed, select the message you want to read to display its contents in the Preview pane.

3. To display a message in its own window, double-click the message.

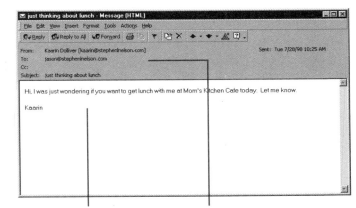

This is the message text.   This area lists the message sender, recipients, and subject description.

Display Another Message

1. Display a message.

2. Click the Next Item button to display the next message.

3. Click the Previous Item button to display the previous message.

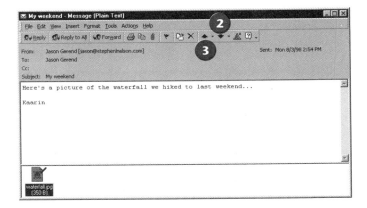

Printing Messages

You can easily print messages as long as your computer connects to a printer or to a network with a printer.

TIP

The Print toolbar button. *If you want to print only one copy of a message and want to use your default printer, you don't have to choose the File menu's Print command. You can click the Print toolbar button instead.*

TIP

Print options. *The Print dialog box also includes options for printing special kinds of messages, such as a message in HTML format or a message that has an attachment.*

Print a Message

1. Display or select the message.

2. Choose Print from the File menu.

3. Optionally, select the printer you want to use from the Name drop-down list box.

4. Select Memo Style from the Print Style list box.

5. Specify how many copies you want in the Number Of Copies box.

6. Click OK.

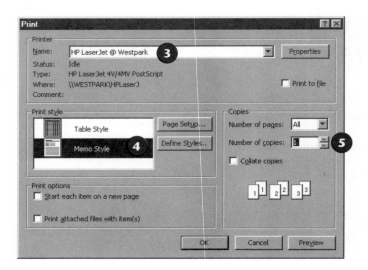

Replying to Messages

You can easily reply to messages you receive. All you do is click the Reply or Reply To All toolbar buttons, and then supply your new message text.

SEE ALSO

See "Sending Messages" on page 34 for information on sending a message.

TIP

Reply to a message with an attachment. *When you reply to a message with an attachment, Outlook doesn't include another copy of the attachment. It just lists the name(s) of the file(s) attached to the original message.*

Reply to a Message

1. Select or display the message to which you want to reply.

2. Click the Reply toolbar button to reply to the sender only, or click the Reply To All toolbar button to reply to the sender and other recipients.

3. Type any new message text.

4. Click the Send toolbar button to send your message.

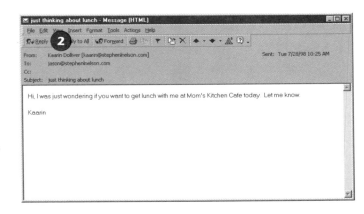

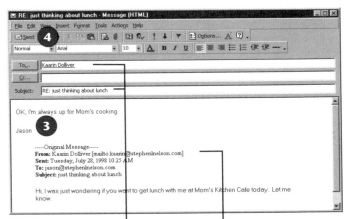

Outlook fills in the To and Subject text boxes for you when you reply to a message.

Outlook includes a copy of the message to which you're replying.

Forwarding Messages

If you receive a message that you think other people should see, you can forward copies of the message to them.

TIP

Forward messages with attachments. *When you forward a message with an attachment, Outlook includes the attachment.*

TIP

Customize forwards and replies. *To tell Outlook how to display the original message text when forwarding or replying to messages (or to tell Outlook not to include the original message text at all), display your Inbox and choose Options from the Tools menu. Click the Preferences tab, and then click E-Mail Options. Use the On Replies and Forwards drop-down list boxes to customize how Outlook handles forwards and replies.*

Forward a Message

1 Display the message you want to forward.

2 Click the Forward toolbar button.

3 Type the name of the person to whom you want to forward the e-mail message in the To text box. Or click the To button to open your Address Book.

4 Type any new message text.

5 Click the Send toolbar button.

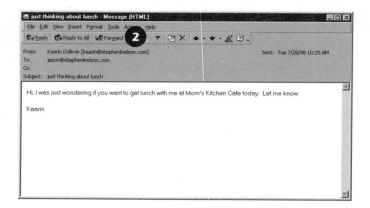

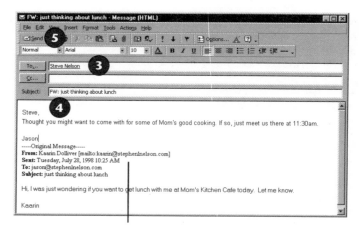

Outlook automatically includes a complete copy of the message you're forwarding.

Opening Message Attachments

You aren't limited to receiving only textual messages from people. You can also receive files in messages. Outlook calls these files attachments.

TIP

Open unwieldy attachments. *Outlook can read just about all types of attachments, but many mail servers can't, so they must recode attachments in order to pass them along. When you receive a recoded attachment, the message body probably says it has a file attached, but you see only a jumble of code. To decode the attachment, save the entire message as a text file and then open the message file using WinZip or a decoding utility such as Wincode.*

SEE ALSO

See "Customizing Internet E-Mail" on page 188 for information on sending attachments in different formats.

Open a Message Attachment

1 Display the message with the attachment.

2 Double-click the attachment icon.

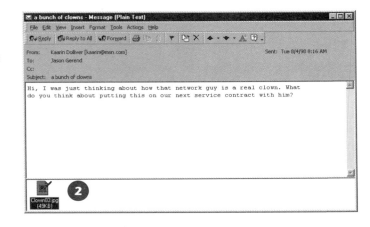

3

Working with Attachments

You may want to save attachments and then open them using other applications. Outlook, however, provides several tools you can use to work with attachments without first opening another application.

Save a Message Attachment

1. Display the message with the attachment.

2. Right-click the attachment icon.

3. Choose Save As from the shortcut menu.

4. Specify where you want the attachment saved by selecting a folder from the Save In drop-down list box.

5. Specify a new name for the attachment if you can't or don't want to use the current name in the File Name text box.

6. Click Save.

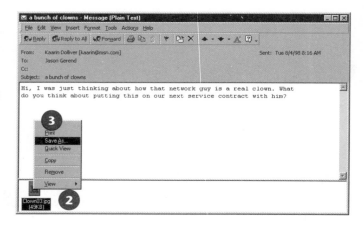

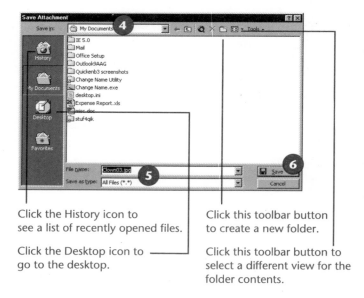

Click the History icon to see a list of recently opened files.

Click the Desktop icon to go to the desktop.

Click this toolbar button to create a new folder.

Click this toolbar button to select a different view for the folder contents.

Open an attachment in the Preview pane. *If you have a message displayed in the Preview pane, click the paper-clip button on the Preview pane to display a pop-up list of files attached to the message. To open or save an attachment, select it from the list. Specify whether you want to open the attachment or save it in the dialog box that Outlook provides.*

Open an attachment. *When you tell Outlook you want to open or print an attachment, Outlook asks Windows to open the attachment with the appropriate application. Windows usually knows which application to use, but if it doesn't know, it asks you to identify the appropriate application.*

Print a Message Attachment

1. Display the message with the attachment.

2. Right-click the attachment icon.

3. Choose Print from the shortcut menu.

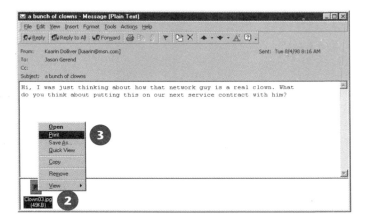

Sending Messages

Once you understand how to receive and read messages, you'll find it very easy to send them. In essence, all you have to do is provide an e-mail name or fax number for the recipient, and then type your text.

TRY THIS

Check that name. *If you don't remember how to spell a person's name, type the first few letters of the first or last name in the To text box and press the Tab key. When Outlook recognizes what you're typing, it fills in the rest of the name and underlines it. If Outlook doesn't underline the name, it means that Outlook did not find a match or found more than one match. Click the Check Names button to have Outlook display a list of the matches it found.*

TRY THIS

Fax a new contact. *If you're sending a fax to someone not in your Contacts list, just type the fax number in the To text box.*

Create and Send a Message

1 Click the Inbox icon on the Outlook Bar.

2 Click the New Mail Message toolbar button or the down arrow next to it for the New Fax command.

3 Type the name of the person to whom you want to send your message in the To text box. To send the message to more than one person, separate the names with semicolons.

4 Optionally, type the names of the people to whom you want to send courtesy copies in the Cc text box.

5 Type a brief message description in the Subject text box.

6 Type your message text.

7 Click the Send toolbar button to send your message, or click the down arrow next to the Send button and choose a specific mail account to send the message with (Internet Only installation).

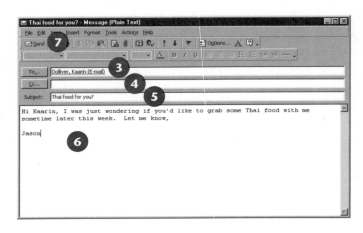

Moving and Copying Message Text

With Outlook you can move and copy message text within a Message window, between different Message windows, and between different application windows.

TIP

Copy text. *To copy text, hold down the Ctrl key while dragging the selection to the new location.*

TIP

Move text between applications. *Moving and copying text by dragging it with the mouse is called drag-and-drop editing. All of the Microsoft Office applications, as well as most other applications, allow drag-and-drop editing.*

TIP

Copy and Paste toolbar buttons. *To copy text from messages you receive, you may need to use the Copy and Paste toolbar buttons.*

Move Text Within a Message

1 Select the text you want to move.

2 Click the text selection, and then drag it to the new location.

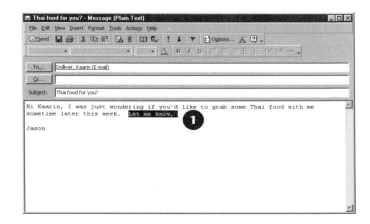

Move Text Between Messages

1 Open the message containing the text you want to move.

2 Open the message in which you want to place the text.

3 Resize and arrange the two Message windows so that both are clearly visible on your screen.

4 Select the text you want to move from the first message.

5 Click the text selection, and then drag it to the new location in the second message.

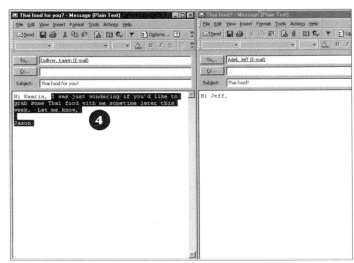

Formatting Message Text

Outlook allows you to richly format your message text. Although you need to be careful about doing this— only recipients with e-mail clients that accept richly formatted messages will be able to see all your formatting—the extra formatting can make your messages more attractive and more readable.

TIP

Not everyone will see your formatting. *Don't depend on formatting for emphasis— many people can only view their e-mail messages in plain text and so do not see the formatting you apply.*

SEE ALSO

See "Specifying Message Format" on page 185 for information on formatting messages.

Specify Text Font, Size, and Color

1 Select the text for which you want to specify the font, size, and color.

2 Open the Font drop-down list box, and select a font for the selected text.

3 Open the Font Size drop-down list box, and select a point size for the selected text.

4 Click the Font Color toolbar button, and then click the color you want to use for the selected text.

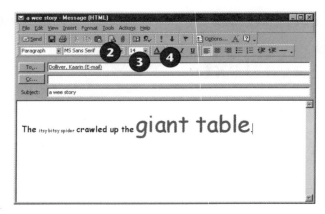

Add special effects to text. *You can control all aspects of a font's appearance by choosing Font from the Format menu. When you do this, Outlook displays the Font dialog box, which lets you specify the font, point size, color, font style, and any special effects—such as strikethrough— for the selected text.*

Remove formatting. *To remove formatting you've added with the Bold, Italic, or Underline toolbar buttons, select the formatted text and then click the toolbar button a second time.*

Specify Other Character-Level Formatting

1. Select the text you want to format.

2. Choose the Formatting toolbar button that applies the character formatting you want:

   ◆ Click Bold to bold the selected text.

   ◆ Click Italic to italicize the selected text.

   ◆ Click Underline to underline the selected text.

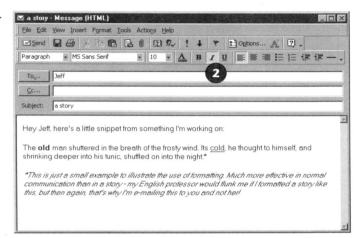

3

Formatting Message Paragraphs

Although most of the formatting you'll apply to messages concerns individual characters, words, and sentences, you can also format paragraphs by specifying how you want them aligned, by turning selected paragraphs into bulleted lists, and by indenting paragraphs.

TIP

List items. *Each paragraph you select becomes a list item after you click the Bullets or Numbering toolbar button.*

TRY THIS

Eliminate bullets. *To convert a list into regular paragraphs, select the list and then click the Bullets or Numbering toolbar button again.*

TIP

The Numbering toolbar button. *The numbering toolbar button only appears if you use HTML or Microsoft Outlook Rich Text to compose messages.*

Specify Paragraph Alignment

1 Select the paragraph you want to left align, center, or right align.

2 Choose the Formatting toolbar button that aligns the paragraph in the way you want:

- ◆ Click Align Left to align the selected paragraph against the left edge of the Message window.
- ◆ Click Center to center the selected paragraph.
- ◆ Click Align Right to align the selected paragraph against the right edge of the Message window.

Create a List

1 Select the paragraphs you want to turn into a list.

2 Choose the Formatting toolbar button that creates the list you want:

- ◆ Click Bullets to create a bulleted list.
- ◆ Click Numbering to create a numbered list.

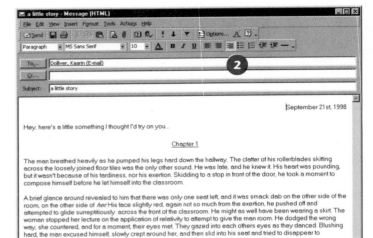

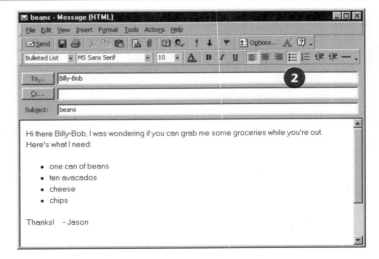

Change Paragraph Indentation

1 Select the text you want to indent or unindent.

2 Choose the Formatting toolbar button that indents the paragraph in the way you want:

◆ Click Increase Indent to indent the paragraph.

◆ Click Decrease Indent to decrease the paragraph indentation.

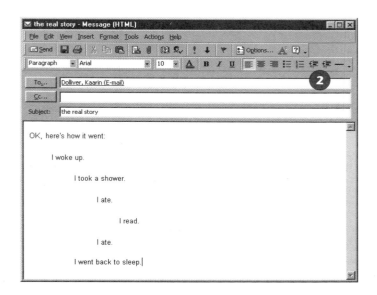

Inserting Files in Messages

You can insert files in your messages in either of two ways: you can attach a file to a message (in this case, the file remains intact inside the message), or you can insert the text contents of a file in a message.

TRY THIS

Insert a shortcut to a file.
If you use Microsoft Outlook Rich Text format, you also have the option of inserting a shortcut to a file in a message. This option keeps the message size down by not actually inserting the file in the message. When the message recipient double-clicks the shortcut, it opens the original file stored on your computer if the recipient has access to your computer across the network.

Attach a File to a Message

1. Display the message to which you want to attach a file.

2. Click the Insert File toolbar button.

3. Specify the location of the file you want to attach by selecting a folder from the Look In drop-down list box.

4. Select the file you want to attach.

5. Click Insert.

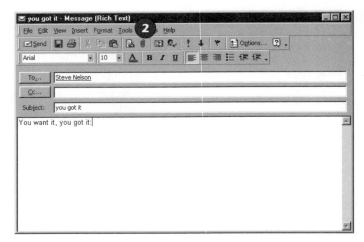

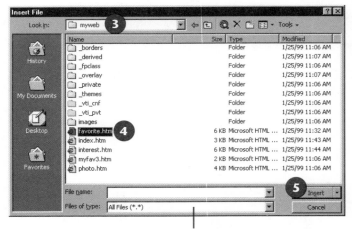

Select HTML files or Text Files from the Files Of Type drop-down list box to display only text files in the list box.

Insert text. *Outlook attempts to insert the text from any file it recognizes. Unfortunately, anything other than a straight text file or simple HTML file usually gets garbled, so if you want to insert a document as a text file, first save it as a .txt or .htm file.*

Insert a Text File in a Message

1. Display the message in which you want to insert a file.

2. Click the Insert File toolbar button.

3. Specify the location of the file you want to insert by selecting a folder from the Look In drop-down list box or clicking one of the folder buttons on the left.

4. Select the file you want to insert.

5. Click the down arrow next to Insert, and choose Insert As Text from the drop-down menu.

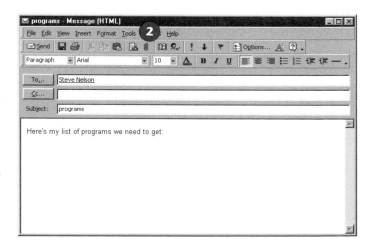

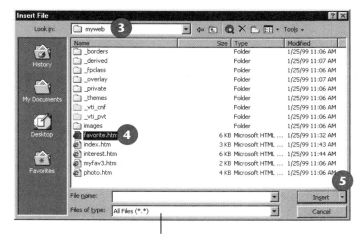

Select HTML files or Text Files from the Files Of Type drop-down list box to display only text files in the list box.

3

Adding Signatures

To quickly add your contact information to e-mail messages, you use signatures. Signatures save you the time of typing your address and phone number at the bottom of every message. With Outlook, you can create and add several different signatures to messages. For example, you can create a business signature for business correspondence and a personal signature for personal correspondence. Or for fun, you can create a signature that includes your favorite saying or a piece of art.

TIP

Signature file formats. *The type of signature file you can create depends on the message format you choose. Signatures created in one format will not be available if you change your message format.*

SEE ALSO

See "Specifying Message Format" on page 185 for information on formatting messages.

Create a Signature

1 Choose Options from the Tools menu.

2 Click the Mail Format tab.

3 Click Signature Picker to display the Signature Picker dialog box, which lists any signatures you've already created.

4 Click New to start the Create New Signature Wizard.

5 Type a name for the new signature.

6 Click Next.

7 Click to place the cursor in the text box, and type your signature text.

8 Click Finish.

9 Click OK.

10 Click OK.

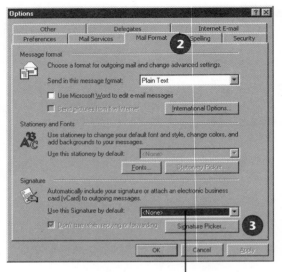

To add a signature you've created to all of your outgoing messages, select the signature from this drop-down list box.

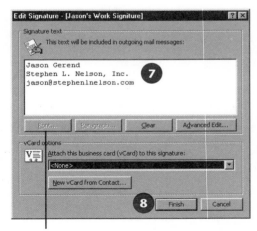

Click Font to change the signature's character formatting.

TIP

Attach a vCard. *To attach a vCard to a signature, select a vCard from the drop-down list box.*

SEE ALSO

See "Exchanging Virtual Business Cards" on page 70 for information on creating vCards.

TIP

Edit signatures. *To edit or delete signatures, display the Signature Picker dialog box and click Edit or Remove.*

Add a Signature to a Message

1 Display the message to which you want to add the signature.

2 Click the Signature toolbar button, and select a signature from the pop-up menu.

3

Inserting Voting Buttons

When you need to conduct a simple survey in your office, you can use Outlook's voting buttons. After you send your query over the network, voting buttons help you easily keep track of the responses you get.

TIP

Where are the buttons? *You can't see the voting buttons when you add them to a message. Only the message recipients see them.*

TIP

Messages with voting buttons. *When you receive a message with voting buttons, the voting buttons appear below the toolbar. To respond, click the applicable voting button. This opens a dialog box that asks you whether you want to send the response now or whether you want to add commentary to your response before you send it. Click the appropriate option button, and then click OK.*

Add Voting Buttons to a Message

1 Create a message that asks a question.

2 Click the Options toolbar button to display the Message Options dialog box.

3 Select the Use Voting Buttons check box, and select the voting buttons you want to use from the drop-down list box.

4 Click Close.

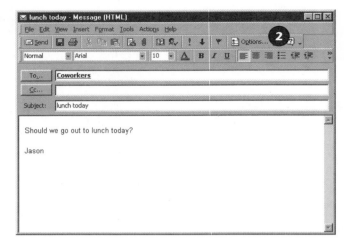

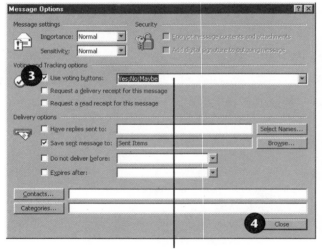

Create your own voting buttons by entering button labels separated by semicolons.

Adding Message Security

Outlook has two ways in which you can increase e-mail security: encrypting and digitally signing messages. You can encrypt messages so that they cannot be intercepted and read by people other than the intended recipients. You can also digitally sign messages so that recipients know they came from you and were not tampered with along the way.

TIP

Obtain a digital ID. *Choose Options from the Tools menu, click the Security tab, and then click Get A Digital ID.*

TIP

Encrypted messages. *You can send anyone a digitally signed message. (Most e-mail clients support secure e-mail.) However, to send someone an encrypted message, the recipient must have a digital ID and you must have a copy of the ID.*

Encrypt a Message

1. Open the message you want to encrypt.

2. Click the Options toolbar button.

3. Select the Encrypt Message Contents And Attachments check box.

4. Click Close.

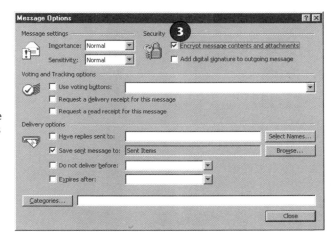

Digitally Sign a Message

1. Open the message you want to digitally sign.

2. Click the Options toolbar button.

3. Select the Add Digital Signature To Outgoing Message check box.

4. Click Close.

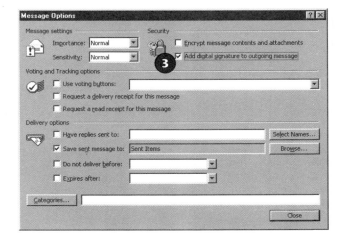

3

Using Outlook's Message-Creation Tools

Outlook provides several handy tools to help you create your messages: You can set message sensitivity and importance, for example, so that some messages stand out in a recipient's Inbox. You can also flag messages that have special characteristics.

TIP

Set defaults. *To set the default message sensitivity and importance for all outgoing messages, choose Options from the Tools menu and click the Preferences tab. Click E-Mail Options, and then click Advanced E-Mail Options. Open the Set Importance and Set Sensitivity drop-down list boxes to choose a default sensitivity and importance other than Normal.*

TIP

Internet Only. *Your Message Options screen will look a little different if you're using the Internet Only configuration of Outlook.*

Set the Message Sensitivity

1. Display the message for which you want to specify a level of sensitivity.

2. Click the Options toolbar button.

3. Open the Sensitivity drop-down list box, and select a sensitivity level: Normal, Personal, Private, or Confidential.

4. Click Close.

Set the Message Importance

1. Display the message for which you want to specify a level of importance.

2. Choose the Formatting toolbar button that sets the importance level you want:

    ◆ High designates a message as very important.

    ◆ Low designates a message as less important.

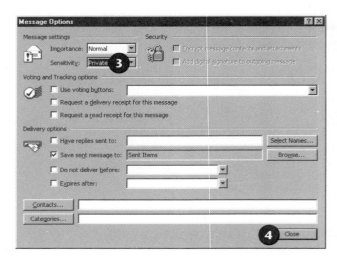

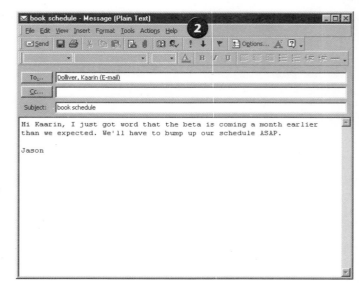

What's that flag? *When you receive a message with a flag, a flag icon appears next to the message in your Inbox.*

Add a Message Flag

1 Display the message you want to flag.

2 Click the Flag For Follow Up toolbar button.

3 Open the Flag To drop-down list box, and select one of the standard flags: For Your Information, No Response Necessary, Forward, and so on.

4 Optionally, open the Reminder drop-down list box, and select a day shown on the calendar.

5 Click OK.

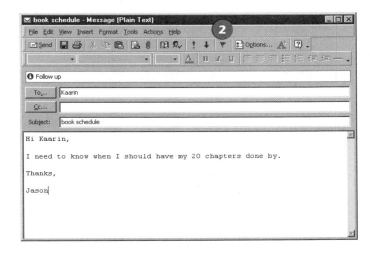

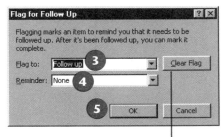

Click here to remove any flags.

Customizing Delivery Options

Outlook has several ways in which you can customize how messages are sent. If you work on a network, you can have the network server send you announcements when your messages have been received or opened. You can also specify a different e-mail address if you don't want replies to a message returned to the address from which you mailed the message. And you can tell Outlook to postpone sending a message or to make a message unavailable for reading after a certain date.

Track a Message

1. Display the message you want to track.

2. Click the Options toolbar button.

3. Select a tracking option:

   ◆ Select the Request A Delivery Receipt For This Message check box to receive a note in your Inbox alerting you that the message has reached the recipient.

   ◆ Select the Request A Read Receipt For This Message check box to receive a note in your Inbox alerting you that the recipient has opened the message.

4. Click Close.

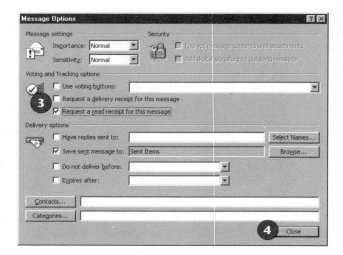

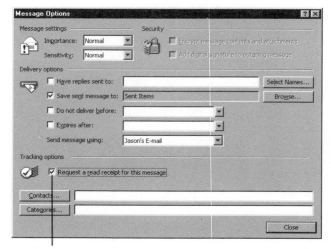

Select this check box to receive an e-mail when your message has been opened (Internet Only screen).

Postpone the Delivery of a Message

1. Display the message you don't want to deliver immediately.

2. Click the Options toolbar button.

3. Select the Do Not Deliver Before check box.

4. Click the down arrow, and select a date to deliver the message from the drop-down calendar.

5. Click Close.

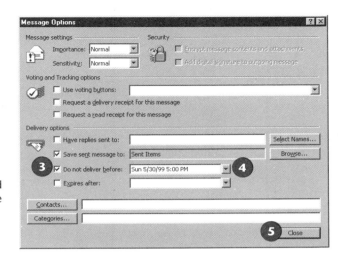

Add Message Expiration

1. Display the message you want to make unavailable after a certain date.

2. Click the Options toolbar button.

3. Select the Expires After check box.

4. Click the down arrow, and select the date after which you want the message to expire from the drop-down calendar.

5. Click Close.

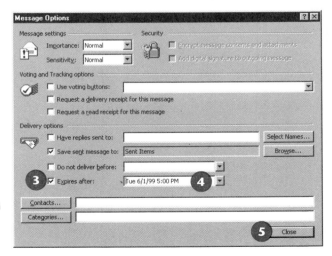

Delivering Your E-Mail Messages

After you create your e-mail messages, you may need to send them by connecting to an online service. (Note that you probably don't need to do anything special to send e-mail messages if you connect to a network with an Exchange server.)

TIP

Look in the Outbox. *To view a message in the Outbox, open the message by double-clicking it. When you close the Message window, the message will return to the Outbox, but it will not deliver unless you open the message again and click the Send toolbar button.*

TIP

Sent but not delivered. *Your Outbox folder shows only those e-mail messages you've sent but not yet delivered. To view the messages you've delivered, display your Sent Items folder.*

View Your Outbox

1 Click the My Shortcuts group on the Outlook Bar.

2 Click the Outbox icon to see your outgoing messages.

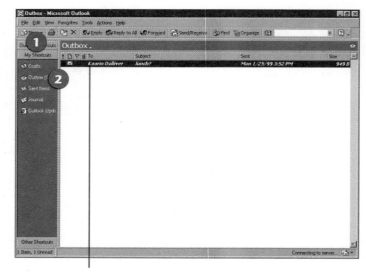

Messages in italics are ready to be delivered.

Send e-mail with a specific account. *If you have more than one e-mail account and want to receive or deliver a message using a particular account, choose Send And Receive from the Tools menu and then select the account. Otherwise, Outlook delivers the message using the first account that is capable of sending messages to the recipient using the address properties you specified for the recipient.*

Deliver Your New Messages

1 Click the Send/Receive toolbar button.

2 Outlook may prompt you to complete whatever sign-on procedures are required to connect to the provider.

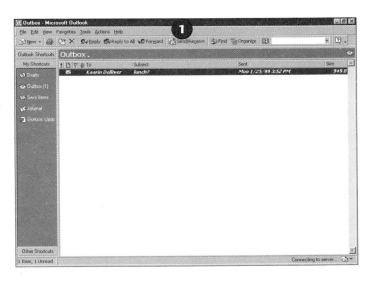

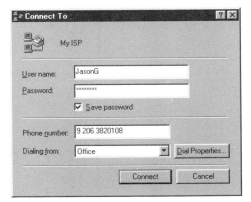

A generic dial-up account log-in dialog box.

4

4

Working with Contacts

Anyone who works with other people needs to stay in touch with those people. This means creating some type of system that tracks information about people and businesses. And the information has to be easy to retrieve and work with. Microsoft Outlook provides such a system with its Contacts feature. Here you can enter contacts in a database and track important information including names and addresses, phone numbers, and e-mail addresses.

Contacts goes far beyond mimicking a card file of names and addresses, however. You can use Outlook's Contacts folder to create and maintain a database, make phone calls through automatic dialing, use e-mail and record contacts on the World Wide Web, and import information from other applications, such as Microsoft Schedule +, to create a new Contacts list. You can even change the appearance of a Contacts list. Whether you are maintaining a list of Girl Scout leaders in your area or vice presidents of a Fortune 500 company, Outlook's Contacts folder makes keeping track of these people easy.

Adding Contact Items

The first step in building a contacts database is adding individual items to your Contacts folder. Adding these items is simple, although slightly time-consuming, because you end up collecting quite a bit of data about each contact.

TRY THIS

Enter two names. *You can enter two names in the first name field by including the word "and" or an "&" between the names like this: Michael & Jenny.*

Add a Contact

1 Click the Contacts icon on the Outlook Bar to display your Contacts folder.

2 Click the New Contact toolbar button.

3 Type the contact's name in the Full Name text box.

4 Type the name of the contact's business in the Company text box.

5 Type street, city, and state address information in the Address text box.

6 Type the contact's phone numbers in the phone and fax text boxes.

7 Type the contact's e-mail address in the E-Mail text box.

8 Type the contact's Web page uniform resource locator (URL) in the Web Page Address text box.

9 Click the Save And Close toolbar button.

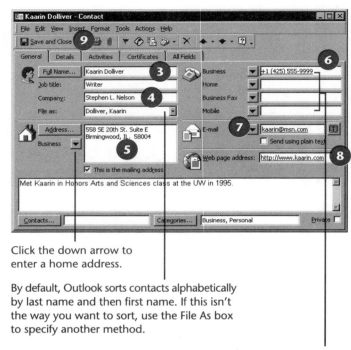

Click the down arrow to enter a home address.

By default, Outlook sorts contacts alphabetically by last name and then first name. If this isn't the way you want to sort, use the File As box to specify another method.

Outlook provides more than one phone number text box so you can enter and describe all of a contact's phone numbers: business, home, fax, and so on.

TIP

No text in phone fields.
Always enter phone numbers as numbers, such as (919) 555-3245, rather than letters, such as (919) THE-SHOW, or the automatic phone dialer will not work properly.

TIP

Missing contacts. *If you can't see your contacts after you've added them, you may have a filter applied to your Contacts folder.*

SEE ALSO

See "Using Filters" on pages 170–171 for information on removing filters.

Collect Personal Information About a Contact

1 Create a new contact or open an existing one.

2 Click the Details tab.

3 Type the contact's department in the Department text box.

4 Type the contact's office location or number in the Office text box.

5 Type the contact's nickname and the contact's spouse's name in the Nickname and Spouse's Name text boxes.

6 If you know the contact's birthday or anniversary dates, type that information in the Birthday and Anniversary text boxes.

7 Click the Save And Close toolbar button to save the contact details information. Alternatively, click the General tab to return to the tab showing the name and address information for the contact.

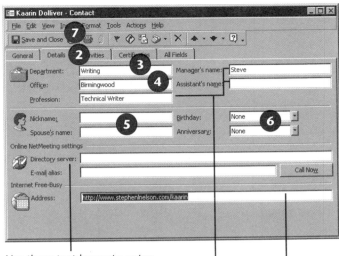

Use these text boxes to enter information for conducting an Internet meeting with the contact using Microsoft NetMeeting.

Use the Profession, Manager's Name, and Assistant's Name text boxes to enter additional professional information about the contact.

If your contact's iCalendar free/busy information is published on the Web, enter the URL here. (Internet Only version.)

4

Updating Contact Items

As the people you know change positions, employers, or addresses, you'll want to update their listings in your Contacts folder.

TIP

Enable in-cell editing. *If Outlook doesn't allow you to make changes directly to a contact's card, choose Current View from the View menu and Customize Current View from the submenu. Click Other Settings, and select the Allow In-Cell Editing check box.*

TRY THIS

See more details. *To view more contact details on the cards, choose Current View from the View menu and Detailed Address Cards from the submenu.*

Edit a Contact Item Using a Card

1. Select the contact item you want to edit.

2. Click the field you want to edit, and make your changes.

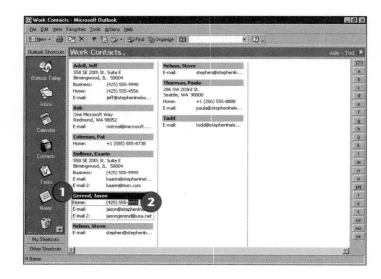

Edit a Contact Using the Contact Dialog Box

1. Double-click the contact you want to open.

2. Make the necessary changes.

3. Click the Save And Close toolbar button.

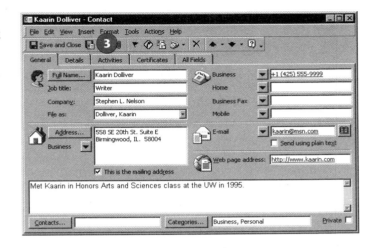

Delete a Contact

1. Select the contact you want to delete.

2. Click the Delete toolbar button.

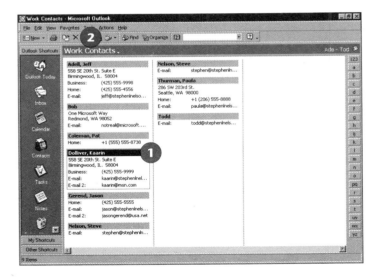

Creating Distribution Lists

You can easily send one e-mail message to a whole list of people without having to manually specify each person by creating a distribution list. Then all you have to do is send the e-mail to the list, and everyone receives it.

TIP

Lists within a list. *Sometimes it's handy to have a list contain another list or lists within it. For example, you could add a "Friends" list to a "Family" list to create a new "Friends and Family" list.*

Create a Distribution List

1. Click the Distribution List toolbar button.

2. Type a name for the list in the Distribution List Name box.

3. Click Select Members.

4. Choose which address list to look in.

5. Select the name of the person you want to add to your list, or type the name.

6. Click Add to add the person to the distribution list.

7. Click OK.

8. Click the Save And Close toolbar button.

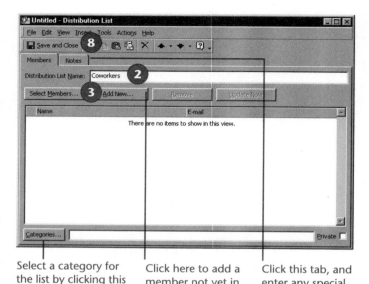

Select a category for the list by clicking this button and selecting the desired categories.

Click here to add a member not yet in Contacts.

Click this tab, and enter any special notes in the text box provided.

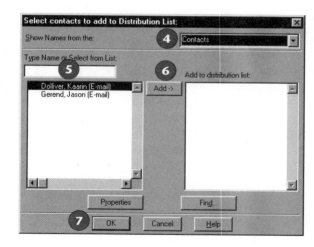

TIP

TIP

Be careful when using distribution lists. *It wouldn't do to write an e-mail with complaints about your boss to your "Friends" list if you accidentally added your boss to the list. Also, some people find it impersonal to receive a nonbusiness form letter, so use lists sparingly.*

TIP

About personal distribution lists. *When a recipient receives a message you sent using a personal distribution list, every name on the list appears in the Message window. This means you can't keep the members of a personal distribution list secret from other members.*

Use Distribution Lists

1. Click the New Mail Message toolbar button from your Inbox to open the New Message window.

2. Click the To button to open the Select Names window.

3. Choose the Address List where the distribution list is stored.

4. Select the distribution list, and then click To.

5. Click OK.

6. Type a subject in the Subject text box.

7. Type your message in the message text box.

8. Click the Send toolbar button to send your message.

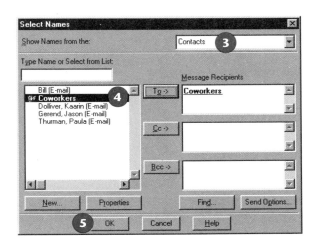

Printing Contact Information

You can print contact information as you can with each of the other Outlook folders and item types.

 Phone Directory Style

TIP

Print preview. *To see how your printed cards will look, click Preview in the Print dialog box.*

TIP

Outlook prints the current view. *Outlook will print only the information about your contact that is displayed in the current view. If you want to print other information about your contact, you must first change the view you're in. For information about changing the Contacts folder's view, see pages 68 and 166.*

Print a Contact

1. Select the card you want to print.

2. Click the Print toolbar button.

3. Indicate how you want Outlook to print the selected item's information in the Print Style box.

4. Click the Only Selected Items option button to print only the highlighted item. Alternatively, click the All Items option button to print all the contacts in your Contacts folder.

5. Click OK.

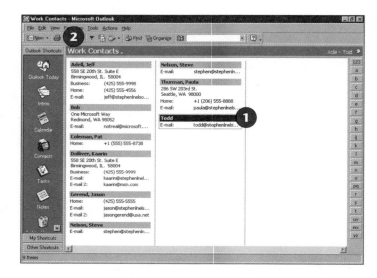

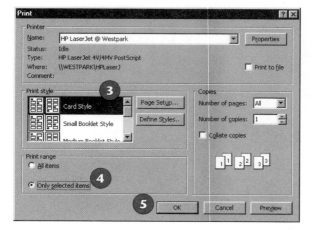

Right-click for help. *If you have a question about what a box or button on the Page Setup dialog box does, right-click the box or button.*

Change the Page Setup

(1) Click the Print toolbar button.

(2) Click Page Setup.

(3) Indicate whether you want Outlook to break to a new page for each letter of the alphabet by clicking one of the Sections option buttons.

(4) Change the typeface used to print the contact information by clicking the Headings and Body Font buttons.

(5) Click OK, and then click OK again to print.

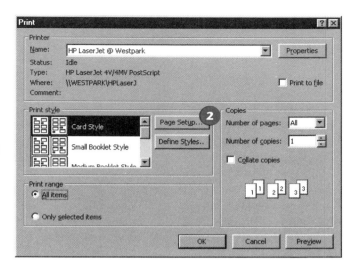

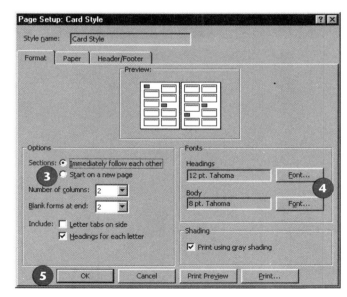

Telephoning Contacts

Because more personal and professional business than ever takes place over the telephone, Outlook offers you a variety of tools for managing this side of Contacts. Using Outlook, you can automatically dial a number, create a list of numbers you frequently call, and even create a list of speed-dial numbers. Keep in mind that to make any telephone calls, you must be sure that your modem is working properly.

TIP

A quick way to get to the Call Contact menu. *From the Contacts folder, click the arrow on the Autodial toolbar button to get to the Call Contact menu.*

Call Someone Not on the Contacts List

1 Choose Call Contact from the Actions menu.

2 Choose New Call from the submenu.

3 Type the number you want to call in the Number text box.

4 Click Start Call, and then pick up the phone and click Talk.

5 When you're finished talking, click End Call and hang up the phone.

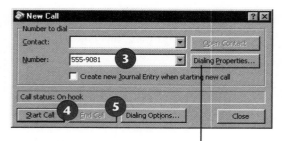

Click Dialing Properties to set dialing options such as your dialing location, an outside access number, area code, and any area code rules your local area may have.

Call Someone on the Contacts List

1. Select the contact you want to call.

2. Choose Call Contact from the Actions menu.

3. Select the phone number you want to dial for the contact from the submenu.

4. Optionally, select the Create New Journal Entry When Starting New Call check box.

5. Click Start Call.

6. Pick up the phone, and click Talk.

7. When you're finished talking, click End Call and hang up the phone.

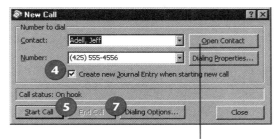

Click Open Contact to display the contact item.

Using Speed Dialing

Outlook lets you use speed dialing with the telephone numbers you've stored in your Contacts folder. For example, you can create a list of frequently called numbers that you can then dial with a couple of mouse clicks. You can also easily redial numbers you've just called.

TIP

Make local calls in a different area code. *To make a local call to a different area code using Windows 98, make sure you have your Dialing Properties and Area Code Rules set up properly. If you have Windows 95, you'll have to manually change your location in Dialing Properties to the area code you want to dial before you dial the number.*

TIP

Add to the Speed Dial list. *To add a contact to your Speed Dialing list, enter the contact's name in the Name box and select the appropriate number for the contact from the Phone Number drop-down list.*

Create a Speed Dial List

1. Choose Call Contact from the Actions menu.

2. Choose New Call from the submenu.

3. Click Dialing Options.

4. Type the name of a person or business you call frequently in the Name text box.

5. Type the person's phone number in the Phone Number text box.

6. Click Add.

7. Click OK.

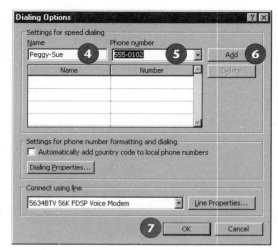

Dial a Speed Dial Number

1. Choose Call Contact from the Actions menu.

2. Choose Speed Dial from the submenu.

3. Select the phone number you want to call.

4. Click Start Call.

5. Pick up the phone, and click Talk.

6. When you're finished talking, click End Call and hang up the phone.

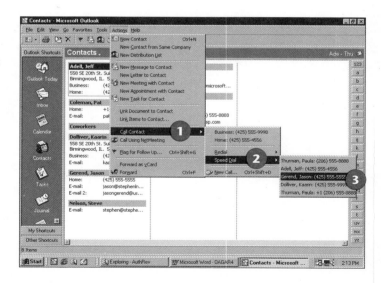

Redial a Phone Number

1. Choose Call Contact from the Actions menu.

2. Choose Redial from the submenu.

3. Select the phone number you want to call.

4. Click Start Call.

5. Pick up the phone, and click Talk.

6. When you're finished talking, click End Call and hang up the phone.

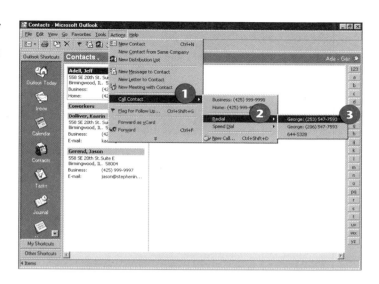

TIP

Delete infrequently used numbers. *You'll want to delete phone numbers from the Speed Dial list when you no longer regularly dial the numbers. If you don't do this, you'll clutter the Speed Dial submenu with numerous unneeded or seldom-used phone numbers.*

Remove a Phone Number from the Speed Dial List

1. Choose Call Contact from the Actions menu.

2. Choose New Call from the submenu.

3. Click Dialing Options.

4. Select the phone number you want to delete.

5. Click Delete.

6. Click OK.

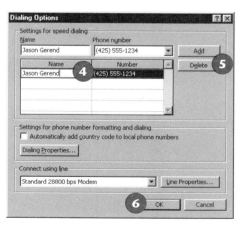

Mapping Contacts

If you have an Internet connection, you can map out any address in your Contacts folder using Microsoft Expedia Maps. This makes it considerably easier to get where you're going.

Map an Address

1. In the Contacts folder, double-click the contact you would like to map.

2. If you would like to map an address other than the contact's business address, click the arrow next to the Address box and select the appropriate address.

3. Click the Display Map Of Address toolbar button to connect to the Internet and display a map of the specified location in Microsoft Internet Explorer.

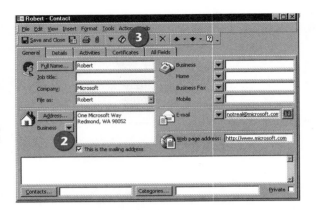

Click here to enlarge the map.

Click here to zoom in and out.

Use the Map Mover arrows to move your map around.

Change your printer's properties. *To print a map in color or at a higher dpi, choose Print from the File menu. Select your printer from the Name drop-down list box, and then click Properties to bring up your printer's Properties window. Change the settings you want, and click OK.*

Print Your Map

1 Map the address of the location to which you want to get directions.

2 Click the Print link to display a larger, printer-friendly version of your map.

3 Choose Print from the File menu.

4 Specify the number of copies you want, and then click OK.

5 Click Internet Explorer's Back toolbar button to return to your map after you're finished printing.

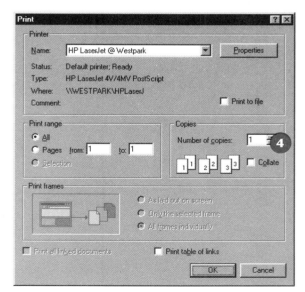

4

Customizing Your Contacts Folder

You can customize the way Outlook's Contacts folder and contact items work. You can, for example, view your Contacts folder as a phone list. And you can specify the bits of information, or fields, you want Outlook to display—and those you don't.

View Your Contacts in a Phone List

1. Choose Current View from the View menu.

2. Choose Phone List from the submenu.

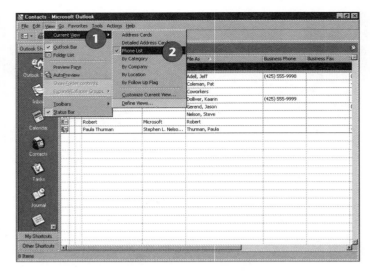

Show or Hide Empty Fields in a Card View

1. Choose Current View from the View menu.

2. Choose Customize Current View from the submenu.

3. Click Other Settings.

4. To show empty fields, select the Show Empty Fields check box. To hide empty fields, clear the Show Empty Fields check box.

5. Click OK.

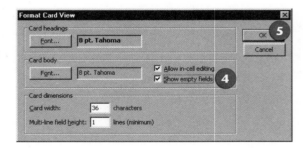

Importing a Contacts List

If you've already created a Contacts list using Microsoft Schedule+ or another program, you won't want to re-create a new Contacts list from scratch. Fortunately, you don't have to. You can import Contacts lists from Schedule+ and several other programs.

TIP

No Import And Export command. *Click the down arrow at the bottom of the File menu to display any hidden commands.*

Import a Contacts List

1. Choose Import And Export from the File menu.

2. Select Import From Another Program Or File from the list box.

3. Click Next.

4. Select the type of format or type of file you want to import from the list box.

5. Click Next.

6. Type the name of the file you want to import in the File To Import text box. Or click Browse to find it.

7. Click Next. Continue to click Next to select the destination folder for the imported file and those portions of the file you want to import.

8. Click Finish to import the file.

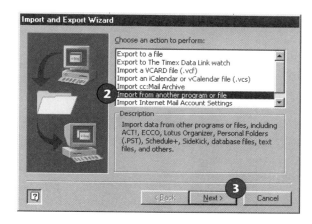

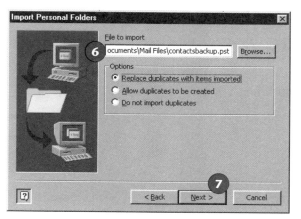

Exchanging Virtual Business Cards

A quick and easy way to exchange contact information with other Outlook users is by exchanging electronic business cards. You can create an electronic business card from any contact and attach the vCard to a mail message. The recipient can then save the information as a contact in his or her own Contacts folder.

Jason
Gerend.vcf

Send a vCard

1. Display your Contacts folder.

2. Select the contact you want to send as a vCard.

3. Choose Forward As VCard from the Actions menu.

4. Fill out the To and Subjects fields, and then type your message.

5. Click the Send toolbar button when you're finished.

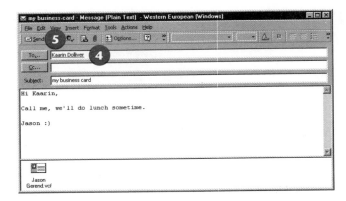

Receive a vCard

1. Open the message containing the vCard by double-clicking the message in the Inbox window.

2. Double-click the attached vCard to open it.

3. Make any necessary changes to the contact, and then click the Save And Close toolbar button to save the new contact to your Contacts folder.

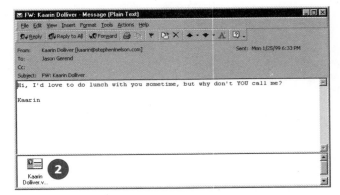

5

Using the Address Book

Microsoft Outlook's Address Book allows you to access the lists you use to store information about your contacts. These lists usually include e-mail addresses (sometimes called e-mail aliases), but they can also include telephone and fax numbers, mailing addresses, and other types of contact information.

The Address Book can actually work with several separate Address Book lists, depending on the services you have installed on your computer. If you're working on a computer connected to a network running Microsoft Exchange server, Outlook's Address Book provides a list of the people on the network to whom you can send e-mail messages. This list of names and e-mail addresses is called the Global Address List. If you're using Outlook's Contacts folder to store contact information, the Address Book provides this list of your contacts and their e-mail addresses and fax numbers. If you used Outlook's predecessor, Microsoft Exchange, Outlook also lets you use Exchange's list of names, e-mail addresses, and fax numbers. This list is called the Personal Address Book. If you're using Outlook's Contacts folder to store contact information, the Address Book provides this list of your contacts and their e-mail addresses and fax numbers. (Note, however, that if your aren't working on a network and don't have any other address book lists, you probably won't need to use the Address Book very much because you can easily work with contacts using the Contacts folder as described in Section 4.

Displaying the Address Book

You can easily display the Address Book's lists of names and e-mail addresses by choosing Address Book from the Tools menu.

TRY THIS

Quick access. *In some of Outlook's folders, you can quickly open the Address Book by clicking the Address Book toolbar button.*

TIP

Select names. *When you click the Address Book toolbar button in a New Message window, or when you click To or Cc, Outlook displays the Select Names dialog box, which lists the names in your Address Book.*

View an Address Book List

1 Choose Address Book from the Tools menu.

2 If you have more than one Address Book list, select the appropriate list of names, addresses, and fax numbers from the Show Names From The drop-down list box.

◆ Select the Contacts entry to see a list of the contacts described in Outlook's Contacts folder.

◆ Select the Personal Address Book entry to see a list of contacts you created using Microsoft Exchange.

◆ Select the Global Address List entry to see a list of the contacts to whom you can send e-mail on a local area network that includes a Microsoft Exchange server.

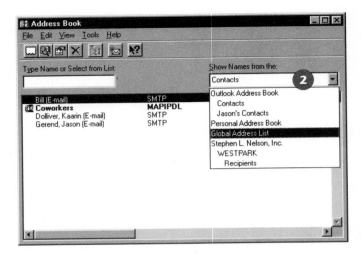

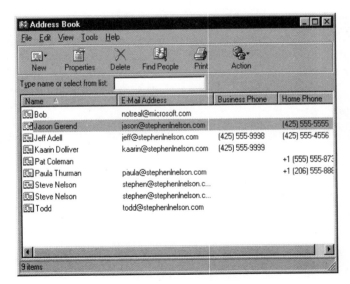

This is what the Internet Only version of Outlook's Address Book looks like.

Internet Only. *If you have more than one Address Book list and you installed the Internet Only version of Outlook, the Show Names drop-down list box is called the Look In drop-down list box.*

View the Details of an Address Book List Entry

1 Display the Address Book window.

2 Select an Address Book list from the Show Names From The drop-down list box.

3 Select the list entry for which you want to view the details.

4 Click the Properties toolbar button.

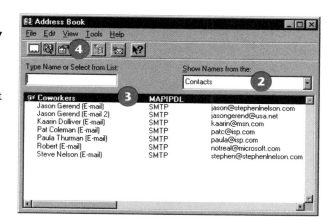

Finding Addresses

Using the Address Book is an easy way to find the names of people to whom you want to send e-mail.

Find a Name in an Address Book List

1 Display the Address Book window.

2 Select an address list from the Show Names From The drop-down list box.

3 Click the Find or Find Items toolbar button.

4 Type the name or part of the name you want to find in your Address Book.

5 If Outlook provides you with other text boxes for entering more information about the person, enter as many details about the contact as you can remember.

6 Click OK or Find Now. Outlook displays any names from your Address Book that match your entry.

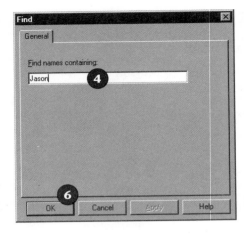

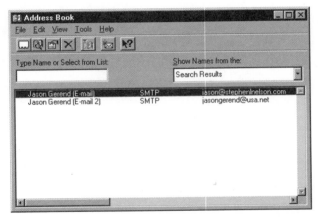

TIP

Missing directory services.
*If you don't have directory
services available in your
Address Book window, click the
Start button, choose Find, and
then choose People.*

TIP

Call the person. *Although
directory services are a neat
tool for finding long-lost
friends, the best way to find
someone's e-mail address is
to call up the person and ask
for it.*

TIP

Don't give up. *A person may
be listed on one directory
search service and not on
another, so don't give up if you
have no luck on the first try.*

TIP

Find people. *To find people
on the Web (using the
Corporate or Workgroup
installation), choose Services
from the Tools menu and click
Add to install the Microsoft
LDAP Directory service.*

Find People on the World Wide Web

1. Display the Address Book window.

2. Click the Find toolbar button.

3. Select a directory service from the Look In drop-down list box.

4. Type the person's name in the Name text box.

5. Enter as much of the person's e-mail address as you know in the E-Mail text box.

6. Click Find Now. If you are not currently logged on to the Internet, Outlook prompts you to do so.

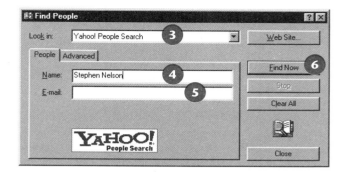

5

Adding Entries to Your Personal Address Book

Although the Contacts folder has largely replaced the Personal Address Book, it is still possible and occasionally useful to add entries to an old Personal Address Book, if you have one.

TIP

Internet Only version of Outlook. *You probably won't have a Personal Address Book with the Internet Only version of Outlook. In this case, all contacts simply go into the much more capable Contacts folder.*

TIP

Change your default address list. *To change your default address list for personal addresses, open your Address Book and choose Options from the Tools menu. Select the address list you want for your default from the Keep Personal Addresses In drop-down list box, and then click OK.*

Add an Entry to Your Personal Address Book

1. Display the Address Book window.

2. Click the New Entry toolbar button.

3. Select the type of entry you want to create from the list box.

4. Select Personal Address Book for the entry location.

5. Click OK.

6. Type the person's name.

7. Fill out the address or mailbox fields required by the type of address you selected.

8. Optionally, click the Business and Phone Numbers tabs to fill in the person's business address and phone numbers.

9. Click OK.

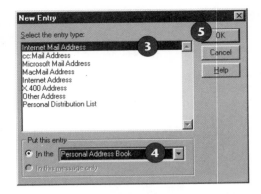

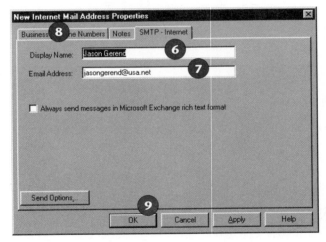

Updating Your Address Book Lists

When people move, change jobs, or just change e-mail services and telephone numbers, you'll want to update their information in your Address Book. Fortunately, this is easy to do with Outlook.

TIP

Delete e-mail Address Book list entries. *To remove an old address entry you no longer need, select the entry from the list and click the Delete toolbar button.*

TIP

The Add To Personal Address Book command. *If the Contacts folder is your default for personal addresses, Outlook will not add an address to the Personal Address Book when you click Add To Personal Address Book, but will instead add it to the Contacts folder.*

Edit an Address Book Entry

1. Display the Address Book window.

2. Select the list with the e-mail entry you want to change from the Show Names From The drop-down list box.

3. Double-click the entry you want to change.

4. Make your changes in the Properties dialog box that Outlook displays.

5. Click OK.

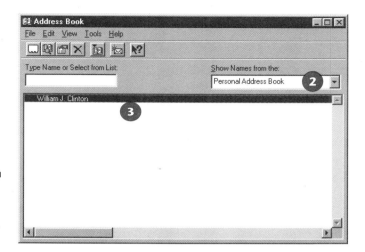

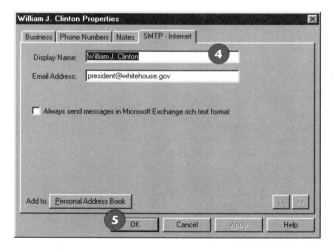

Outlook displays different Properties dialog boxes for different types of Address Book entries.

Using Your Address Book for E-Mail

Once you've recorded the names of the people to whom you want to send e-mail messages, you can use your Address Book to select recipients or distribution lists when you want to send an e-mail message.

TIP

Send a courtesy copy. *To send someone a carbon copy, or courtesy copy, of a message, click Cc and then select the Address Book list you want to use from the Show Names From The drop-down list box. Double-click the name of the person to whom you want to send a courtesy copy of the message.*

TIP

Send a blind carbon copy. *To send someone a blind, or secret, carbon copy of a message, choose Bcc Field from the View menu. Then click the Bcc box to select a blind carbon copy recipient.*

Use the Address Book to Select an E-Mail Recipient

1. Display your Inbox.

2. Click the New Mail Message toolbar button.

3. Click To to display the Select Names dialog box.

4. Select the Address Book list you want to use from the Show Names From The drop-down list box.

5. Double-click the names of the people to whom you want to send the message.

6. Click OK to return to the Message window.

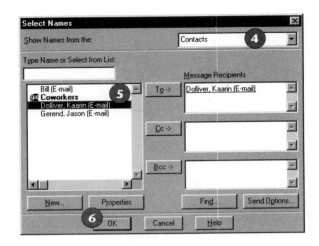

A word of warning about blind carbon copies.

When you send someone a blind carbon copy, the other recipients should not be able to see that you sent the other person a copy. Unfortunately, however, the blind carbon copy recipient is often not hidden as it should be, so it's risky to send blind carbon copies.

Send a Message to a List

1 Display your Inbox.

2 Click the New Mail Message toolbar button.

3 Click To to display the Select Names dialog box.

4 Select the Address Book list you want to use from the Show Names From The drop-down list box.

5 Double-click the Personal Distribution List you want to receive the message.

6 Click OK to return to the Message window.

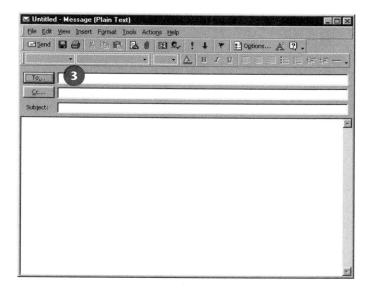

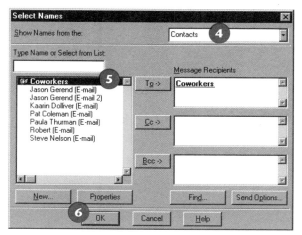

Sorting Your Address Book

You can control some aspects of the Address Book's operation. For example, you can indicate which Address Book list you want to see first. You can also rename and reorganize your Personal Address Book or specify a different Personal Address Book.

Specify a Default Address Book List

1 Display the Address Book window.

2 Choose Options from the Tools menu.

3 Select the Address Book list you want to appear by default from the Show This Address List First drop-down list box.

4 Click OK.

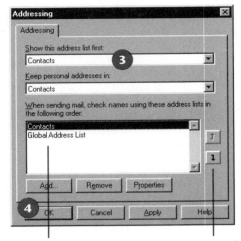

You can use this list box to specify which Address Book lists you want to use first for checking names.

To move an Address Book list up or down, select it and then click the Up Arrow or Down Arrow button.

Customize Your Personal Address Book

1 Display the Address Book window.

2 Choose Options from the Tools menu.

3 Select the Personal Address Book entry.

4 Click Properties.

5 Optionally, change the Personal Address Book's name by typing a new name or editing the name shown in the Name text box.

6 To select a different Personal Address Book, click Browse.

7 Click OK twice to return to the Address Book window.

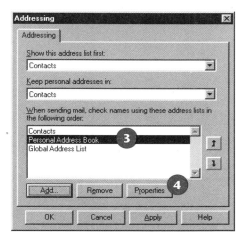

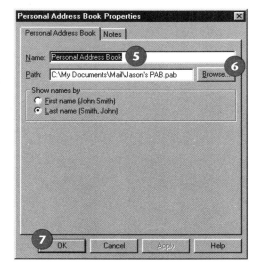

Using Newsgroups

Microsoft Outlook 2000 comes with a special newsreader program, Microsoft Outlook Express, which you can use to read and post messages to newsgroups. Newsgroups, like e-mail, are a highly popular form of Internet communication. Newsgroups work much like bulletin boards: people post messages for anyone stopping by to read. Some newsgroups are private and only accessible by employees of a certain company or members of a certain club. Other newsgroups are publicly accessible, much like a bulletin board you might find at your local library.

Internet newsgroups differ from bulletin boards in one important way, however. Most newsgroups are fairly specialized. There are thousands of Internet newsgroups on every subject imaginable, ranging from professional societies to fan clubs and hobby enthusiasts to support and advice groups. People post a variety of information to these groups, such as advertising goods and services, asking questions, and responding to issues. You can use Outlook Express to work with newsgroups and become a participant yourself.

Getting Started with Newsgroups

To begin working with newsgroups, you need to start Outlook Express and download a list of available newsgroups. The Outlook Express program window looks a little different than the Outlook window, but it works in much the same way.

Start Outlook Express

1 Choose News from the Go menu. This displays the Outlook Express window, which resembles Outlook Today.

2 Click an icon to work with the newsgroup part of Outlook Express.

◆ Click Create A New News Message to post a new message on a newsgroup.

◆ Click Read News to read and post messages to newsgroups you've already subscribed to.

◆ Click Subscribe To Newsgroups to download a list of the newsgroups available on a server.

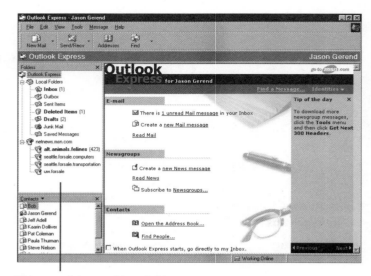

This pane lists your News folders, news servers, and the newsgroups you've subscribed to.

Display the List of Available Newsgroups

1. Select the news server on which you want to view a list of the available newsgroups.

2. Click Newsgroups.

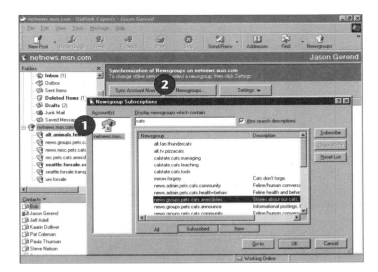

Viewing and Subscribing to Newsgroups

After you've downloaded the list of newsgroups available to you, you can display a list of the messages posted to individual newsgroups. You can then begin reading the messages posted to the newsgroup. If you find a newsgroup that looks interesting to you, you can subscribe to the newsgroup so that you can easily access the newsgroup and read new messages posted to it.

TIP

Connect to the Internet.
If Outlook Express does not display a list of the messages posted to the newsgroup when you click Go To, you are not connected to the Internet. Click the Connect toolbar button to connect and download a list of the newsgroup's message headers.

TIP

Search newsgroup descriptions. *Select the Also Search Description check box to search newsgroup descriptions and names.*

View a Newsgroup's Messages

1 Select your news server.

2 Click Newsgroups.

3 To display a list of newsgroups on a certain topic, enter a keyword in the text box. Outlook Express lists all the newsgroups that include this keyword in their name.

4 Select a newsgroup whose messages you want to preview.

5 Click Go To. Outlook Express displays a list of the messages posted to the newsgroup you selected.

6 To read a message, select one from the list. Outlook Express News displays the message text in the Preview pane.

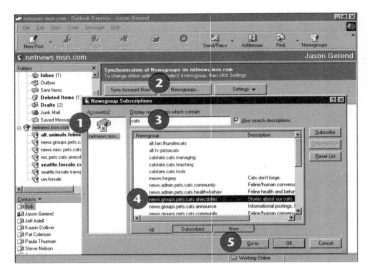

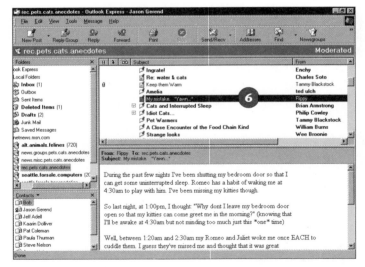

Subscribe to a Newsgroup

1. Select a news server.

2. Click Newsgroups.

3. Select the newsgroup from the list.

4. Click Subscribe.

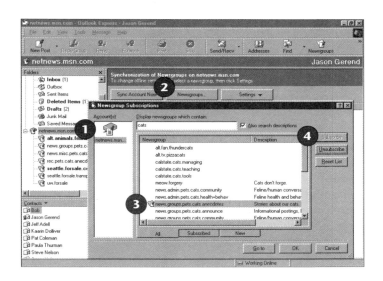

Unsubscribe from a Newsgroup

1. Right-click the newsgroup in the Folder list.

2. Choose Unsubscribe from the shortcut menu.

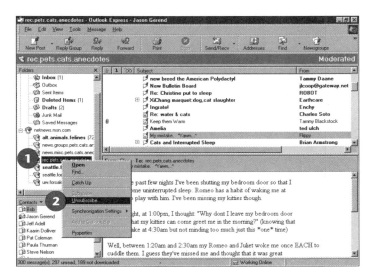

Synchro-nizing Newsgroup Messages

Outlook Express allows you to browse newsgroups both online and offline. To read messages offline, you must first select which messages you want to download and then download the text for those messages.

TIP

Work offline. *To tell your computer that you don't want to be connected to the Internet while you work, choose Work Offline from the File menu.*

TIP

Discussion threads. *If a message has a plus sign beside it, it belongs to a group of messages relating to the same topic, called a discussion thread. You may have to click a message's plus sign to view the other messages in that discussion thread.*

Select Messages to Download

1 Display the list of messages in a newsgroup.

2 Select a message you want to download.

3 Choose Mark For Offline from the Tools menu.

4 Choose one of the submenu's commands for retrieving messages.

◆ Choose Download Message Later to retrieve the text of the selected message.

◆ Choose Download Conversation Later to retrieve the text of all messages in the selected discussion thread.

◆ Choose Download All Messages Later to retrieve the text of all messages in the newsgroup.

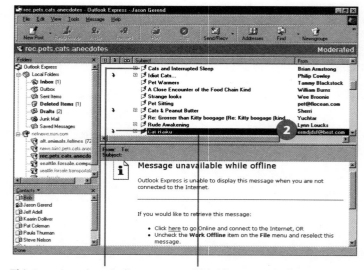

This torn page icon indicates that you have not downloaded the message.

This blue arrow indicates that the message is marked for retrieval.

Change newsgroup offline settings. *To change a newsgroup's offline settings, select your news server in the Folder list, select a newsgroup in the Synchronization Of Newsgroups pane, and click Settings. Choose an option from the drop-down menu.*

Synchronize Messages

1. Select your news server in the Folder list.

2. Click Sync Account Now.

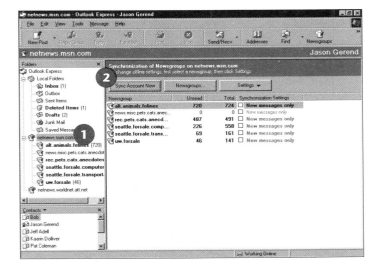

Reading Newsgroup Messages

After you've downloaded the messages you want to read, you can read them offline. Of if you're working online, you're ready to read any message you want. The process of reading messages works the same for both cases. To preview a message, just select the message's heading. This displays the message text in the Preview pane. To expand the view of the message, you can also display the message in its own window.

Display a Newsgroup Message in Its Own Window

1 Select the newsgroup containing the message you want to read from the Folder list.

2 Double-click the message to display the message text in its own window.

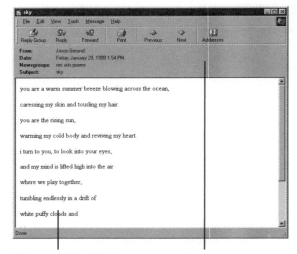

This part of the Message window displays the text of the message.

This part of the Message window lists information about the message: its sender, the newsgroups it was posted to, and the date it was posted.

Working with Attachments

People share many different types of information through newsgroup messages. For example, one of the most popular types of information shared is graphics images. Because figure files cannot be converted to text, it is common for news-group messages to have attachments. Using Outlook Express, you can view and save message attachments.

TIP

Split the attachments.
When attachments are too large to send in a single message, people split the attachments between messages. To combine the messages that include parts of an attachment, select the messages from the Message List. (You can usually identify the messages that go together because people label them (1/5, 2/5, 3/5 and so forth.) Then choose Combine And Decode from the Message menu.

Save a Message Attachment

1. Display the message with the attachment in its own window.

2. Right-click the attachment, and choose Save As from the shortcut menu.

3. Use the Save In drop-down list box to specify where you want to save the attachment.

4. Enter a name for the attachment in the File Name box.

5. Click Save.

6

Posting to Newsgroups

After you have worked with newsgroups for a while and have familiarized yourself with the postings to a newsgroup, you can begin posting messages yourself.

TIP

Post to multiple newsgroups. *To post a message to more than one newsgroup, choose Select Newsgroups from the Tools menu.*

TIP

Reply to a message. *To reply to a message someone has posted, select or display the message and click the Reply toolbar button to send an e-mail to the message author or click the Reply Group toolbar button to post a message to the newsgroup in regard to the original message. Messages and their replies make up a discussion thread.*

TIP

Message won't display. *If a message won't display, either you are working offline and haven't downloaded the message or the message has expired.*

Post a Message

1. Select the newsgroup from the Folder list to which you want to post.

2. Click the New Post toolbar button.

3. Type a message subject in the Subject line.

4. Type the message text.

5. Click the Send toolbar button.

6. If you are working offline, click the Send/Receive toolbar button to deliver the message.

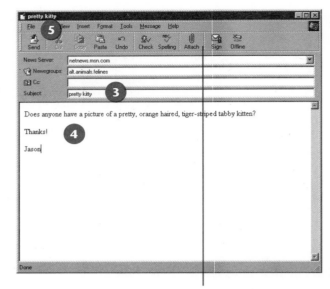

To attach a file to a message, click the Attach File toolbar button.

Using the Calendar

Microsoft Outlook includes a handy, online appointment calendar to help you schedule your days. You can make appointments (such as a visit to the doctor), jot down reminders (such as a note to pick up milk on the way home), and record important annual events (like an anniversary or birthday) with Outlook's Calendar.

If you've worked with other components of Outlook, you'll find the Calendar extremely easy to use. Outlook provides a Calendar folder where you store appointment, event, and meeting items. In most cases, to record appointments, reminders, and events, you simply identify a date and time and then provide a description.

If your computer connects to a local area network and that network includes Microsoft Exchange Server, Outlook also provides a group scheduling feature. With group scheduling, you can schedule meetings for a group of participants by letting Outlook find common open time slots. For example, using Outlook's group scheduling feature, you can discover when members of a project team all have a two-hour time slot open for a project status meeting.

Viewing Your Calendar

Using Outlook's Calendar, you can easily view the appointments and events you have planned. You can find a date and edit the activities scheduled for that day. You can change the view of the Calendar to get an overview of your week's or month's schedule. You can also display your Calendar as a list if you want to find lost calendar items or clean up erroneous items.

Display a Date in the Calendar

(1) Click the Calendar icon on the Outlook Bar to display your Calendar.

(2) Use the arrows on the right and left sides of the Date Navigator calendars to display the month you want.

(3) Select the date you want to display by clicking it on the Date Navigator.

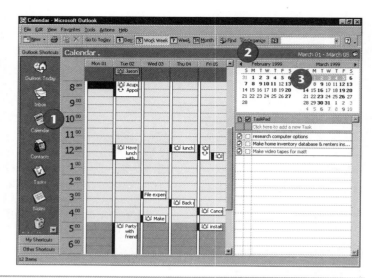

Change the Calendar View

(1) Display your Calendar.

(2) Click one of the View buttons on the toolbar to view different time periods.

◆ Click Day to view one day's schedule by hour.

◆ Click Work Week to view one work week's schedule by hour.

◆ Click Week to view one week's schedule by day.

◆ Click Month to view one month's schedule by day.

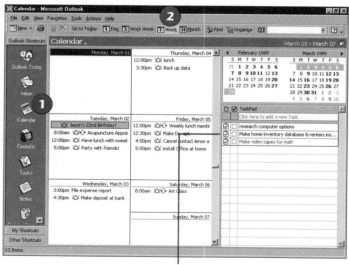

To make more room for your Calendar, you can narrow the Date Navigator and TaskPad by dragging this bar to the right.

Month view. *When you view a whole month in your Calendar, the Date Navigator and TaskPad disappear.*

Save as web page. *You can save your Calendar as a Web page by choosing Save As Web Page from the File menu.*

View Your Calendar Items in a List

1 Display your Calendar.

2 Choose Current View from the View menu.

3 Select a different view.

◆ Choose Active Appointments to view a list of all your appointments and events.

◆ Choose Events to view a list of all-day events.

◆ Choose Annual Events to view all-day events that occur regularly each year.

◆ Choose Recurring Appointments to view only appointments and events that reoccur.

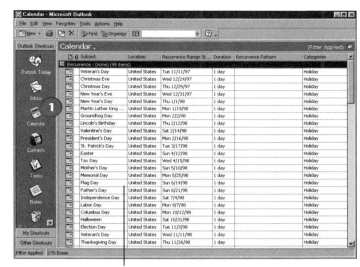

This view lists all the events stored in your Calendar.

Managing Appointments

Outlook appointments start and end on specific dates and at specific times. When you use Outlook, you won't find yourself scheduling a meeting with a customer and a visit to your doctor for the same time slot.

TRY THIS

Another appointment. *To add an appointment to a day you have displayed in your Calendar, select the time frame in which the appointment occurs and type an appointment description directly in the Calendar window. Or double-click the time the appointment begins, and use the Appointment window Outlook displays to describe the appointment in detail.*

Create an Appointment

1. Display your Calendar.

2. Click the New Appointment toolbar button.

3. Describe the appointment in the Subject text box.

4. Enter the date and time that the appointment starts in the Start Time boxes.

5. Enter the date and time that the appointment ends in the End Time boxes.

6. If you won't be available for other meetings during this appointment time, select Busy from the Show Time As drop-down list box.

7. If you don't want other people to be able to see this appointment when they view your Calendar over a network, select the Private check box.

8. Click the Save And Close toolbar button.

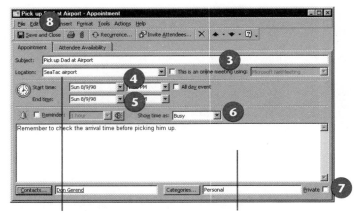

Identify where the appointment takes place, if necessary, in the Location text box.

Describe the appointment more fully, if necessary, in this text box.

Close an appointment. *To close an appointment, click the Close box on the Appointment dialog box. If you haven't saved your changes, Outlook asks if you want to do so before closing.*

May I reschedule? *To reschedule an appointment, change the information in the Start Time and End Time boxes.*

Display an Appointment

1 Display your Calendar.

2 Double-click the appointment you want to review.

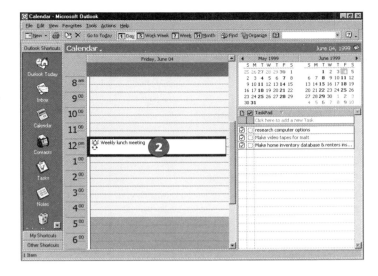

Edit an Appointment

1 Display your Calendar.

2 Double-click the appointment you want to edit.

3 Make changes by replacing text box contents and selecting or clearing check boxes.

4 Click the Save And Close toolbar button.

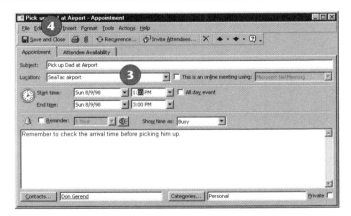

Working with Reminders

If you work with your computer all day, you may want your computer to remind you of upcoming appointments—with either message boxes you read or audible warnings you hear.

Sounds

Request an Appointment Reminder

1 Display your Calendar.

2 Double-click the appointment you want to be reminded about.

3 Select the Reminder check box.

4 Specify how far in advance you want to be reminded in the Reminder box.

5 Click the Reminder Sound button.

6 Select the Play This Sound check box.

7 To select a different Reminder sound, click Browse and use the Reminder Sound File dialog box to locate the sound file you want to use.

8 Click OK.

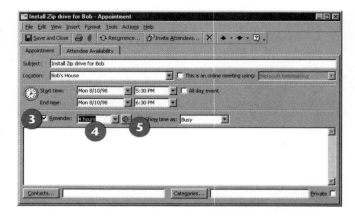

Open the item. *If you have questions about a Reminder, just open the item.*

Change Reminder options. *By default, Outlook plays the Reminder sound and displays the Reminder box when a message comes due. To change these settings, or to select a different default Reminder sound, choose Options from the Tools menu and click the Other tab. Click Advanced Options, and then click Reminder Options.*

Respond to a Reminder

1 Click Dismiss to close the Reminder box.

2 Click Snooze to reschedule the Reminder for a specified time in the future.

3 Click Open Item to open the item to which this Reminder refers.

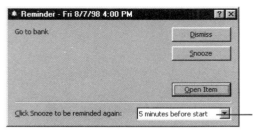

If you click Snooze, indicate how long you want to postpone the Reminder by selecting an entry from this drop-down list box.

7

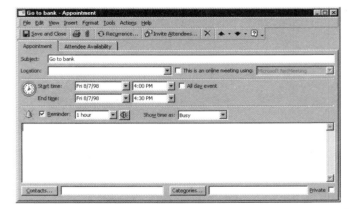

Deleting Appointments

When you cancel an appointment, you'll want to remove the appointment from your Calendar by deleting the item.

TIP

No confirmation. *Outlook doesn't provide a confirmation message box when you choose Delete from the shortcut menu. So be careful not to accidentally delete appointments you want to keep.*

TIP

Delete recurring appointments. *If you tell Outlook to delete a recurring appointment, Outlook asks if you want to delete only the single instance of the appointment or all occurrences.*

Delete an Appointment

1. Display your Calendar.

2. Select the appointment you want to delete.

3. Click the Delete toolbar button.

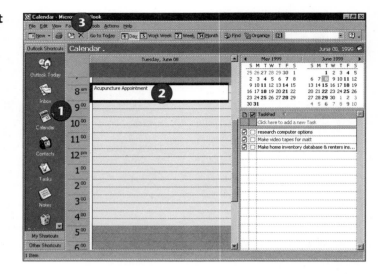

Printing Calendar Items

Outlook makes it easy to print individual appointment information as well as daily, weekly, and monthly Calendar information.

TIP

Another way to print. *You can also print an individual appointment by displaying it in its own window and choosing the File menu's Print command.*

TIP

Page Setup. *Click Page Setup to change the font, paper size, and margins or to add a header or a footer.*

Print an Appointment

1. Select the appointment.

2. Click the Print toolbar button.

3. Optionally, select the printer you want to use from the Name drop-down list box.

4. Select Memo Style from the Print Style list box to print only the selected appointment, or select one of the other styles to print your Calendar.

5. If you choose to print your Calendar, use the Print Range boxes to select the range of dates you want to print.

6. Specify how many copies you want to print in the Number Of Copies box.

7. Click OK.

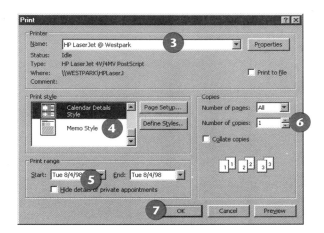

Creating Event Items

Events differ from appointments in that events typically don't preclude other activities. For example, an event such as a family member's birthday is important to remember. But scheduling this event doesn't prevent you from scheduling other appointments or even other events (another person's birthday, for instance) on the same day.

TIP

Events work like appointments. *You work with events in the same basic manner as you work with appointments. For example, you create, display, categorize, and edit events in the exact same way that you do appointments.*

Create an Event

1. Display your Calendar.

2. Click the New Appointment toolbar button.

3. Describe the event in the Subject text box.

4. Identify where the event takes place, if necessary, in the Location text box.

5. Select the All Day Event check box. When this box is checked, Outlook changes the name of the window from Appointment to Event.

6. If you will be available during this event for other appointments, events, or meetings, select Free from the Show Time As dropdown list box.

7. Describe the event more fully in the main text box.

8. If you don't want other people to be able to see this event when they view your Calendar over a network, select the Private check box.

9. Click the Save And Close toolbar button.

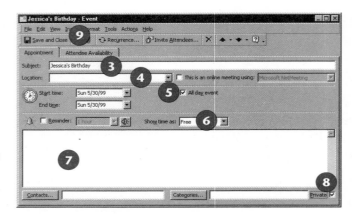

Recurring appointments.
You can create recurring appointments in the same manner as you create recurring events.

See "Viewing Your Calendar" on pages 94–95 for information on displaying your events in a list.

Describe How Often an Event Recurs

1. Display your Calendar.

2. Double-click the event you want to describe as recurring. Outlook displays the Event dialog box.

3. Click the Recurrence button.

4. Indicate how frequently and according to what pattern this event recurs by using the Recurrence Pattern option buttons and boxes.

5. Indicate how far into the future this event will recur by using the Range Of Recurrence option buttons and boxes.

6. Click OK.

7. Click the Save And Close toolbar button.

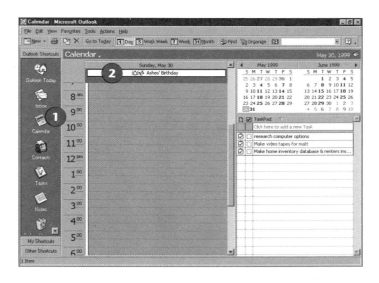

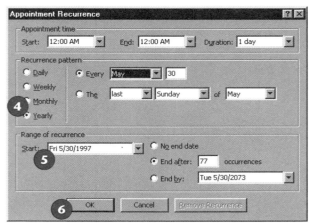

Scheduling Meetings

If your computer connects to a local area network that includes an Exchange server, you can use Outlook to schedule group meetings. Outlook looks for an empty time slot that fits into everyone's schedule by examining Calendars for each of the meeting's participants.

TIP

Schedule over the Internet.
To plan a meeting with someone over the Internet, in the Select Attendees window choose the people or resources who have URLs for their iCalendar information recorded in their contact information. To set up your own publishing location, choose Options from the Tools menu and then click Calendar Options. Click Free/ Busy Options, and enter your web site's URL. To publish your information, choose Send And Receive from the Tools menu and Free/Busy Information from the submenu.

Plan a Meeting

1. Display your Calendar.

2. Choose Plan A Meeting from the Actions menu.

3. Click Invite Others.

4. Double-click the names of participants to add them to the All Attendees list; then click OK.

5. Select a time when the meeting participants are free from the Meeting Start Time and Meeting End Time boxes.

6. Click AutoPick to have Outlook automatically select the next open time slot that works for all the participants.

7. Click Make Meeting.

8. Describe the meeting in the Subject text box.

9. Confirm the meeting date and time in the Start Time and End Time boxes.

10. Click the Send toolbar button.

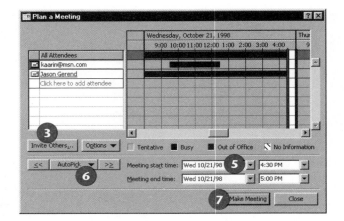

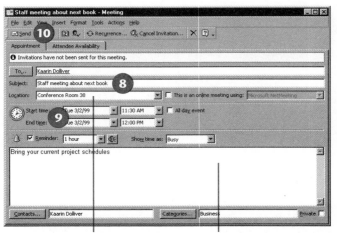

Identify where the meeting takes place, if necessary, in the Location text box.

Describe the meeting more fully, if necessary, in this text box.

Request a Meeting

1. Display your Calendar.
2. Choose New Meeting Request from the Actions menu.
3. Type the names of the participants you want to attend your meeting.
4. Describe the meeting in the Subject text box.
5. Type the meeting date and time in the Start Time and End Time boxes.
6. Click the Send toolbar button.

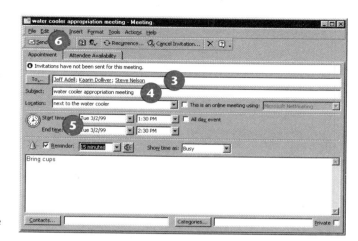

Respond to a Meeting Request

1. Display your Inbox.
2. Double-click the meeting request you want to read.
3. To agree to a meeting, click the Accept toolbar button.
4. If you agree to a meeting, Outlook schedules it in your Calendar.

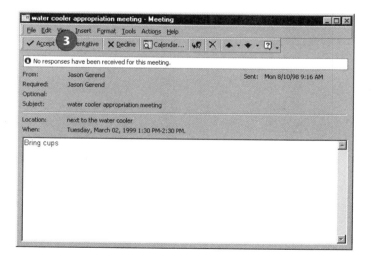

Using Microsoft NetMeeting

NetMeeting is a program that comes as a part of Microsoft Internet Explorer with Outlook 2000. Using NetMeeting, you can conduct meetings with people in real time over the Internet. NetMeeting allows you to hold different kinds of meetings depending on the multimedia capabilities of the participants. If you have a microphone and a sound card, you can conduct audio meetings similar to telephone calls. If you have a video camera attached to your computer, you can send video as well. And you can use NetMeeting's Chat window and Whiteboard to write or sketch messages for others to see. With NetMeeting, you can even share files and applications.

To run NetMeeting, click the Start button, choose Programs, choose Internet Explorer, and then click Microsoft NetMeeting. The first time you run NetMeeting, it takes you through a wizard that sets up NetMeeting. The wizard asks you for some information about yourself that it uses to list you on a directory server. (A directory server is, in essence, a virtual conference room.) The wizard also asks you which server you want to log on to when you start NetMeeting and whether you want to use NetMeeting for personal, business, or adult-only communication. Lastly, the wizard conducts a test of your microphone to optimize the sound quality you record and send.

Once you are set up, you are ready to begin using NetMeeting to hold meetings in cyberspace. As soon as you start NetMeeting and connect to the Internet, the NetMeeting window lists the people currently logged on to your directory server.

The red asterisk indicates that the person is currently in a call.

The gray video camera icon indicates that the person can send video.

The yellow speaker icon indicates that the person can send audio.

To initiate a conversation with someone listed in the NetMeeting window, right-click the person's name and choose Call from the shortcut menu. To initiate a conversation with someone who you know is logged on to the server, but whose name you can't find in the list (and this is quite possible because the list is often very long), click the Call toolbar button. When NetMeeting displays the New Call dialog box, enter the person's e-mail address in the Address drop-down list box. Note that if the person has more than one e-mail address, you must use the one they specified when they set up NetMeeting.

To conduct a meeting and open it to more than one person, tell the people with whom you want to meet when to log on to the server and then choose Host Meeting from the Call menu. Note that only two of the meeting participants can send audio or video and they must send it one at a time.

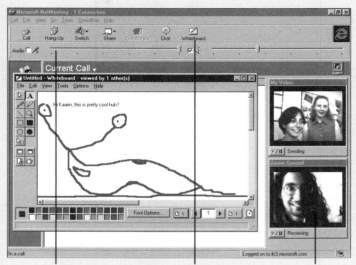

Move these sliders to adjust your recording and playing volume.

Click the Whiteboard toolbar button to display the Whiteboard.

You can also send and receive video.

Using the TaskPad

If you're looking for a simple way to keep track of your task list, you might not need to use Outlook's Tasks folder and its items. Instead, you may be able to get along just fine by using the Calendar folder's TaskPad, which works as a scaled-down version of Outlook's Tasks list feature. The TaskPad lets you easily build and use simple lists of tasks.

SEE ALSO

See Section 8, "Working with Tasks," for information on using the Tasks list.

Add a Task to the TaskPad

1. Click the first row in the TaskPad.

2. Type a brief description of a task.

3. Press the Enter key.

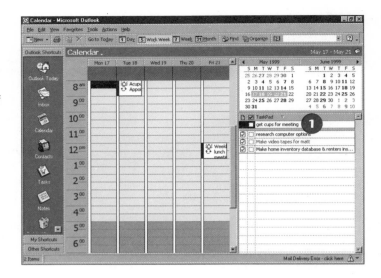

Edit a Task in the TaskPad

1. Click the task you want to edit.

2. Replace the old task description by typing a new one.

3. If you double-click a task description, Outlook displays the Tasks window, which you can use to provide a detailed description of the task.

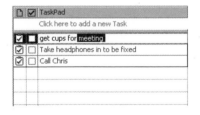

Undo a task check off. *If you inadvertently check off a task that is not completed, just click the box again to remove the check mark.*

Check Off a Task as Complete

① Select the check box to the left of the task you have completed.

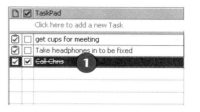

Delete a Task

① Select the task you want to delete.

② Click the Delete toolbar button.

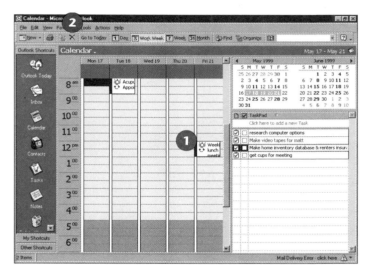

Customizing the Calendar

The Calendar Options dialog box lets you specify what the Outlook Calendar should look like and how it should work.

> **TIP**
>
> **Set a Reminder.** *To tell Outlook to remind you of appointments by default, select the Default Reminder check box. To specify how far in advance you want to be reminded of your appointments, select the length of time from the drop-down list box.*

> **TIP**
>
> **Set free/busy options.** *To specify how Outlook should share your free/busy information, click Free/Busy Options. Use the dialog box to tell Outlook how many months of your free/busy information it can make available to others on the server and how often it should update your free/busy information. You can also specify the URL to post your iCalendar information to on the Internet.*

Specify Your Calendar Work Week

1 Choose Options from the Tools menu.

2 Click the Preferences tab.

3 Click Calendar Options.

4 Select the days of your work week with the Calendar Work Week check boxes.

5 Select the day on which your work week starts from the First Day Of Week drop-down list box.

6 Select an entry from the First Week Of Year drop-down list box to tell Outlook whether you want to count the first week of the year as beginning on January first, regardless of what day of the week it falls on, or whether you want to begin counting with the next full week.

7 Enter your working hours in the Start Time and End Time boxes.

8 Click OK.

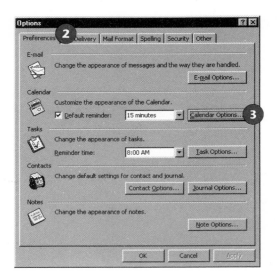

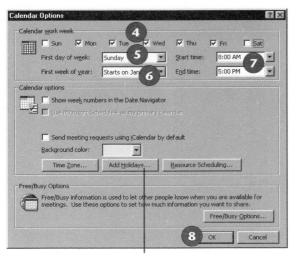

To add national or religious holidays to your Calendar, click Add Holidays.

Process meeting requests automatically. *To process meeting requests automatically, click Resource Scheduling in the Calendar Options dialog box. Select the first check box if you want Outlook to automatically accept meeting requests and enter them in your Calendar. Select the second check box if you want Outlook to automatically decline meeting requests that conflict with other appointments.*

Display a Second Time Zone

1 Choose Options from the Tools menu.

2 Click the Preferences tab.

3 Click Calendar Options.

4 Click Time Zone.

5 Select the Show An Additional Time Zone check box.

6 Enter a name for the second time zone.

7 Select the time zone you want to add.

8 Optionally, select the Adjust For Daylight Saving Time check box.

9 Click OK.

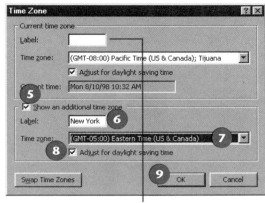

Add a label here to describe your location.

8

Working with Tasks

Tasks are personal or work-related responsibilities that you want to complete and keep track of as you complete them. For example, your task list might consist of personal items, such as shopping for groceries or picking up the dry-cleaning. Your task list might also remind you about tasks you need to accomplish at work, such as preparing a series of reports for a meeting or submitting your presentation to the printer by the end of the day.

Microsoft Outlook lets you take complete control of your task list. For example, you can create a list of tasks and set start and stop dates, and you can customize the list by changing the task priorities. If you're managing a list of tasks at work, you can assign tasks to others and track the progress made on each task. You can also change the way tasks are managed by doing such things as creating a task that recurs every week or month.

Whether you manage a household or a corporation, you're sure to find that the task list you generate will make you more efficient in your work and will probably make getting your work done more satisfying.

Creating Tasks

The first step in working with tasks is creating a task list to keep track of the jobs that need to be done. In the beginning, it's simply a matter of listing tasks and setting dates for starting and completing them.

TIP

Delete a task. *To delete a task, select the task and click the Delete toolbar button.*

TIP

New tasks go on top. *As you add new tasks to your list, they automatically go to the top of the list, regardless of their due date or priority, unless you have the list sorted otherwise.*

Create a Task

1. Click the Tasks icon on the Outlook Bar to display your Tasks folder.

2. Click the New Task toolbar button.

3. Type a task name in the Subject text box.

4. Specify the due date for the task, if there is one.

5. Set a start date for the task, if necessary.

6. Indicate the status of the task if you have already started work on the task.

7. Select a Priority setting for the task.

8. Select the Reminder check box to set a Reminder for the task.

9. Enter the date and time you want to be reminded of the task.

10. Click the Save And Close toolbar button.

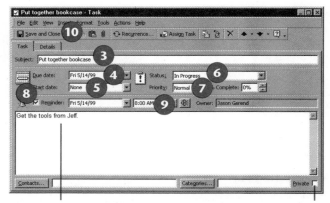

You can type comments about the task here.

Select this check box to make a task private so that others can't see it.

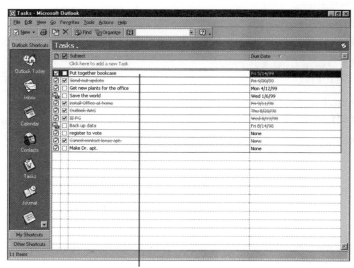

A task displayed in the Tasks list.

TIP

A quick way to add a task.
To quickly add a task directly to your task list, click where it says Click Here To Add A New Task, enter the task subject and due date, and press the Enter key.

TIP

Stop a task from recurring. *Display a task, choose Recurrence from the Actions menu, and then click Remove Recurrence to stop a task from recurring.*

TIP

Skip a recurring task once. *Open a task and choose Skip Recurrence from the Actions menu to skip a recurring task once.*

Create a Task That Recurs

1 Create or display a task.

2 Click the Recurrence button.

3 Specify how often the task recurs by clicking one of the Daily, Weekly, Monthly, or Yearly option buttons.

4 Specify the recurrence pattern.

5 Select start and end dates from the Range Of Recurrence boxes.

6 Click OK.

7 Click the Save And Close toolbar button.

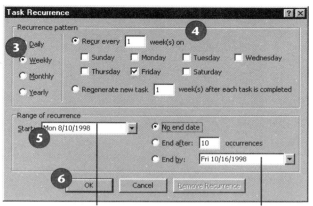

Enter a start date here.   Enter an end date here.

8

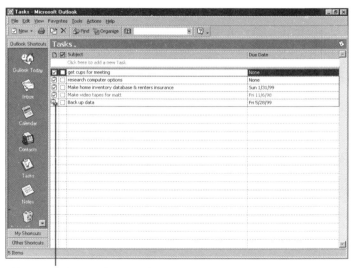

This icon indicates that a task is recurring.

Working with Your Task List

Once you have created a few tasks, you can begin working with the information in your task list: editing task details and checking off tasks as you complete them.

TIP

Double-click to open.
You can also open a task by double-clicking it in the Calendar's TaskPad.

TIP

Sort by Due Date. *You can sort tasks by due date by clicking the Due Date column heading.*

TRY THIS

Sort your list. *If your task list is not sorted, you can move a task up or down the list by selecting the task and dragging it.*

SEE ALSO

See "Sorting Items" on page 168 for information on turning off the sorting feature.

Open a Task

1 Display your Tasks folder.

2 Double-click the task you want to open.

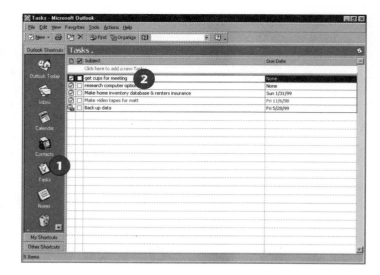

Change the Date a Task Is Due

1. Select the due date of the task that you want to change.

2. Enter a new due date.

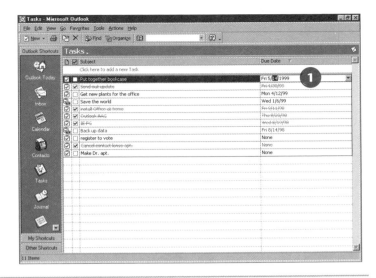

Check Off a Task as Complete

1. Select the task you have completed.

2. Select the check box to the left of the task you have completed.

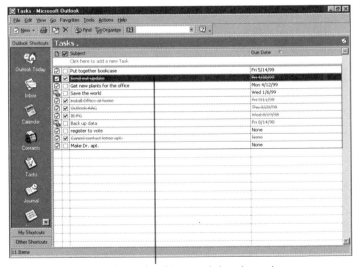

Outlook crosses out the task subject and due date when you check off a task as complete.

8

Updating Task Progress

As you work with Outlook, you'll discover other task-associated options that you may want to make use of. For example, you can carefully track the progress you're making on tasks so that you know exactly how much work you've done and how far you have to go.

In Progress	Thu 8/13/98	75%
Completed	Mon 8/3/98	100%
Not Started	Fri 8/21/98	0%

TIP

Hours become days. *When you enter hour amounts in the Total Work and Actual Work text boxes, Outlook converts them to days based on how many hours per day and per week are in your work week. You can set the number of hours in your work day and work week by choosing Options from the Tools menu and clicking Advanced Options.*

Update a Task's Percentage of Completion

1. Double-click the task you want to update.

2. Enter the percentage of completion in the % Complete box.

3. Click the Save And Close toolbar button.

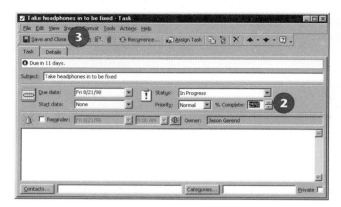

Record Time on a Task

1. Open the task for which you want to record the time spent or the estimated total time.

2. Click the Details tab.

3. Enter the amount of time you think it will take to complete the task in the Total Work text box.

4. Enter the amount of time spent on the task as it is being completed in the Actual Work text box.

5. Click the Save And Close toolbar button.

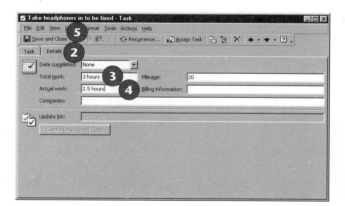

Assigning Tasks

When you assign tasks to people, you send them task requests. The recipients can either accept the task, decline the task, or assign it to someone else. When recipients accept tasks, the tasks get added to their task lists. But even when you assign a task to another person, you can still keep it on your task list to track its progress.

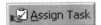

TIP

Assign existing tasks. *Open a task and click the Assign Task toolbar button to assign a task you've already created.*

TIP

Set defaults. *To set Outlook's defaults for tracking assigned task progress, choose the Tools menu's Options command and click the Other tab. Then click Advanced Options and Advanced Tasks.*

Create a Task Request

1. Display your Tasks folder.

2. Choose New Task Request from the Actions menu.

3. Type the name of the person to whom you want to send a task request in the To text box.

4. Type a task name in the Subject text box.

5. Type the date the task is due in the Due Date box.

6. Type the date when the task starts in the Start Date box.

7. Type any instructions associated with the task.

8. Click the Send toolbar button.

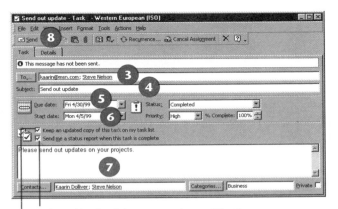

Select this check box to receive notification when the task recipient completes the task.

Select this check box to keep the task on your task list and track the recipient's progress on the task.

Monitoring Task Progress

Outlook makes it easy to monitor the tasks that must be completed and keep track of the progress you and others are making on your tasks.

SEE ALSO

See "Sending Messages" on page 34 for information on creating and sending messages.

Send Task Information to Others

1 Open the task for which you want to send a status report.

2 Click the Send Status Report toolbar button.

3 Type the recipient's name in the To text box.

4 Add any comments.

5 Click the Send toolbar button.

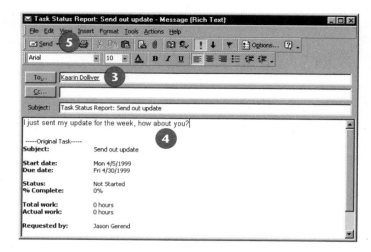

Customizing Your Task List

Once your task list is established and you've mastered some of the basics, such as editing tasks and updating them as you complete them, you can begin working with more advanced features of Outlook Tasks, such as customizing the way your task list looks.

Change the Color of Overdue or Completed Tasks

1. Choose Options from the Tools menu.

2. Click the Preferences tab.

3. Click Task Options.

4. Select a color from the Overdue Tasks drop-down box.

5. Select a color from the Completed Tasks drop-down box.

6. Click OK.

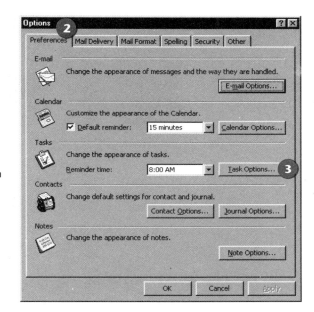

Working with Different Task Views

You can easily change the view of your task list to display your tasks according to the criteria you specify. The table shown here summarizes Outlook's task list views.

TIP

Missing tasks. *If you cannot see all the tasks that are on your task list, you may have applied a special view. Display your task list in the Simple List or Detailed List view. If you still can't see all of your tasks, you may have a filter applied.*

SEE ALSO

See Section 12, "Customizing Outlook," for information on sorting, filtering, and viewing Outlook Folder lists.

Change the View of the Task List

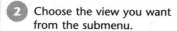 Choose Current View from the View menu.

Choose the view you want from the submenu.

USING THE CURRENT VIEW BOX	
Current View option	**What it does**
Simple List	Lists all tasks and shows which tasks have been completed.
Detailed List	Lists all tasks and shows their status, percent complete, priority, and category.
Active Tasks	Lists tasks that are not yet completed.
Next Seven Days	Lists those tasks scheduled to be completed during the next seven days.
Overdue Tasks	Lists those tasks that are overdue.
By Category	Lists tasks by category.
Assignment	Lists tasks that have been assigned to others.
By Person Responsible	Lists tasks by the person responsible for completing the task.
Completed Tasks	Lists completed tasks.
Task Timeline	Presents a visual timeline of when tasks start and when they are to be completed.

Using the Journal

Microsoft Outlook's Journal organizes Outlook items and, if you choose, Microsoft Office documents chronologically against a timeline. The Journal really amounts to another way of arranging and viewing the information you create and store in Outlook and, optionally, in other Microsoft Office documents.

Most information doesn't lend itself all that well to this timeline-based organization. But there are situations where it comes in extremely handy. You might use the Journal, for example, to record the telephone calls, e-mail messages, tasks, and Microsoft Word documents that you've created for a particular contact or project or that fall into a pre-defined category. In this manner, you could chronologically organize all of the information related to a particular contact, project, or category. Using the Journal, for example, you would more easily be able to find and review all the information related to a contact, project, or category that was generated over the last few months.

Automatically Recording an Activity

You will probably want Outlook to automatically record all events. That way, you have no need to worry whether you might have missed something important. For example, if you create a new Microsoft Access database to track the names and addresses of clients and want a record of that activity, the Journal will automatically record the creation of the database.

TRY THIS

Journal housekeeping. *You can click AutoArchive Journal Entries to display a dialog box that lets you describe when, and how, old entries are removed from your Journal.*

Record an Activity Automatically

1. Choose Options from the Tools menu.

2. Click the Preferences tab.

3. Click Journal Options.

4. Select the check boxes in the Also Record Files From list box next to the Microsoft Office programs that you want automatically recorded in the Journal.

5. Click OK.

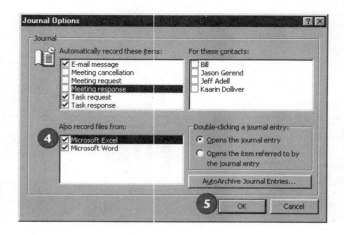

Turn off automatic recording. *To turn off automatic recording, click to clear the check boxes next to the items or programs you no longer want to record automatically.*

Record Items for Contacts Automatically

1 Choose Options from the Tools menu.

2 Click the Preferences tab.

3 Click Journal Options.

4 Select the check boxes in the Automatically Record These Items list box next to the Outlook activities that you want automatically recorded in the Journal.

5 Select the check boxes to indicate those contacts for which you want to record the Outlook items.

6 Click OK.

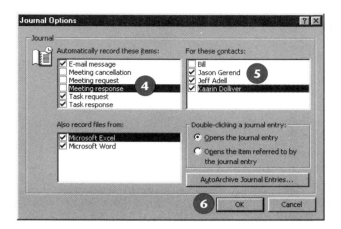

Manually Recording Activities

Not all activities can be automatically recorded in the Journal. For example, tasks and appointments cannot be automatically added to the Journal. To record these items, you must do so manually.

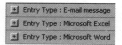

TRY THIS

Pick a date. *If you open the Start Time drop-down list box, Outlook displays the Date Navigator, which you can use to select the start time date.*

TIP

Check names. *Click the Check Names toolbar button to make sure you typed the contact's name correctly. If Outlook does not underline the contact's name when you do so, the name is not in your Contacts folder and you will have to create a new contact.*

Record Any Activity Manually

1. Click the Journal icon on the Outlook Bar under the My Shortcuts group to display your Journal.

2. Click the New Journal toolbar button.

3. Open the Entry Type drop-down list box, and select the type of Journal entry you want to record.

4. If appropriate, identify the contact associated with the activity.

5. If appropriate, identify the activity's start time in the Start Time box.

6. Click the Save And Close toolbar button.

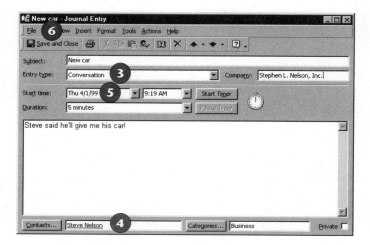

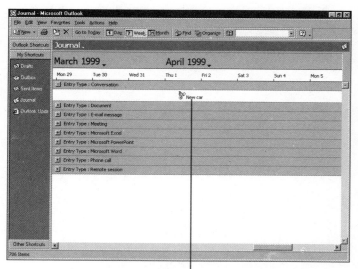

This conversation was manually recorded in the Journal.

Only Office documents can be recorded. *Any Microsoft Office document can be automatically recorded in the Journal. However, documents from other applications (such as Lotus 1-2-3 or Corel WordPerfect) can't.*

See "Viewing Files and File Properties" on page 148 for information on using Outlook to locate files.

Record a File or Outlook Item Manually

1. Use Outlook, Windows Explorer, or the desktop to locate the item or file you want to record.

2. Drag the item or file to the Journal icon on the Outlook Bar.

3. Edit the contents of the Subject and Entry Type boxes if necessary.

4. If appropriate, identify the contact.

5. If appropriate, identify the file or item's start time or duration.

6. Click the Save And Close toolbar button.

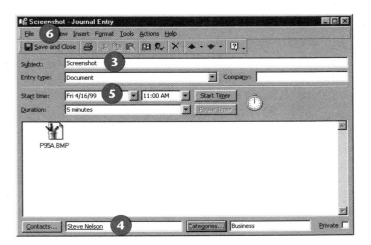

9

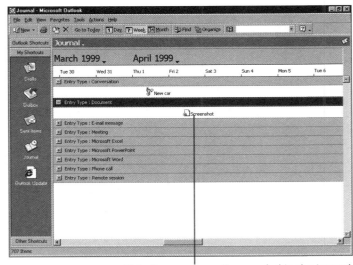

This file was manually recorded in the Journal.

Opening and Modifying a Journal Entry

Journal entries help you keep a record of your activities. Like other Outlook items, these entries can be opened and modified to fit your needs. Once opened, a Journal entry can be edited and then saved and closed.

TIP

Find an entry. *If you have trouble finding a Journal entry, click the Find toolbar button, type some text relating to the entry, and then click Find Now.*

Open a Journal Entry

1. Display your Journal.

2. Click the plus sign next to the Entry Type containing the Journal entry you want to open.

3. Double-click the Journal entry you want to open.

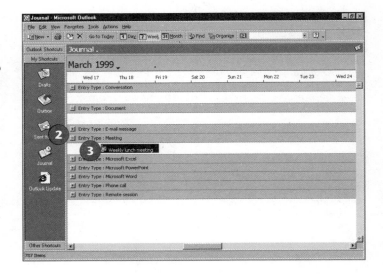

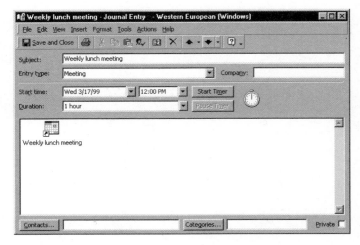

Categorize entries. *You can categorize Journal entries in the same way that you categorize other Outlook items. By categorizing Journal entries, you make it easier to find them later.*

Modify a Journal Entry

1 Display your Journal.

2 Click the plus sign next to the Entry Type containing the Journal entry you want to modify.

3 Double-click the Journal entry you want to open.

4 Modify the Journal entry by selecting the options you want to change.

5 Click the Save And Close toolbar button.

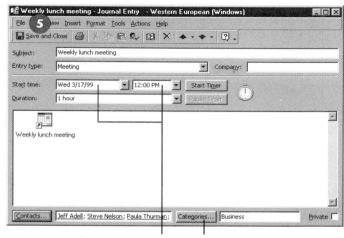

Use these boxes to change the entry's date or time.

Click Categories to recategorize the item.

9

Working with Items Referred to by Journal Entries

You can open the items referred to by Journal entries. In most cases, all you need to do is double-click the Journal entry that refers to the item or document that you want to open. (In effect, the Journal entry works like a shortcut icon.)

TIP

Always open the item.
To always open the item or document to which the Journal entry refers, choose Options from the Tools menu and click the Preferences tab. Click Journal Options, and then click the Opens The Item Referred To By The Journal Entry option button.

Open an Item or Document Referred to by a Journal Entry

1 Display your Journal.

2 Open the Journal entry that refers to the item or document you want to open.

3 Double-click the shortcut icon to the document you want to open.

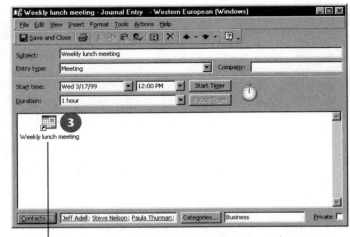

This is an appointment item from Outlook's Calendar.

Open the Contact Referred to by a Journal Entry

1 Display your Journal.

2 Open the Journal entry that refers to the contact you want to view.

3 Double-click any underlined names in the Contacts text box.

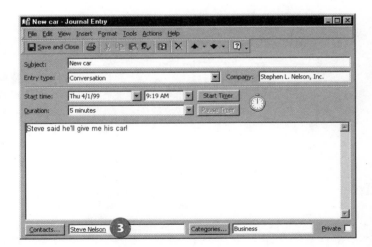

View Journal Entries for a Contact

1 Open the contact with the Journal entries you want to view.

2 Click the Activities tab.

3 Select the type of Journal entry you want to see from the Show drop-down list box.

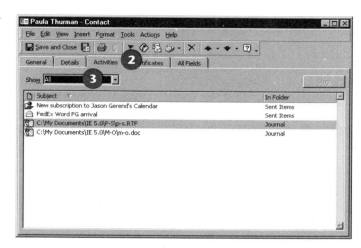

Working with the Journal Entry Timeline

The Journal entry timeline can show you when items were started, saved, sent, modified, or received. Depending upon how you choose to view the timeline, you can easily tell the status of a project with a single glance.

TIP

Same start and end points. *If you choose the same field for your start and end points, the timeline won't show duration for projects.*

Change the Display on the Timeline

1 Choose Current View from the View menu.

2 Choose Customize Current View from the submenu.

3 Click Fields.

4 Select the field that contains the time you want to use as the start point from the Available Date/Time Fields list box.

5 Click Start.

6 Select the field that contains the time you want to use as the end point from the Available Date/Time Fields list box.

7 Click End.

8 Click OK.

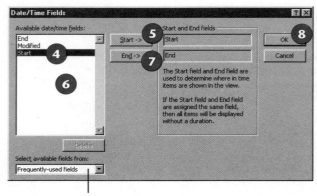

Use this drop-down list box to change the available fields.

Show or Hide Week Numbers

1. Choose Current View from the View menu.

2. Choose Customize Current View from the submenu.

3. Click Other Settings.

4. Select or clear the Show Week Numbers check box.

5. Click OK.

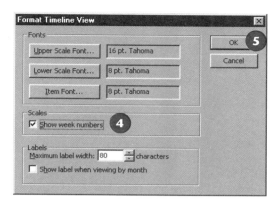

Change the Amount of Time Displayed

1. Click the View button on the toolbar that corresponds to the amount of time you want shown in the Journal:

   ◆ Click Day to view the timeline in hours.

   ◆ Click Week to view the timeline in days.

   ◆ Click Month to view the timeline in days and weeks.

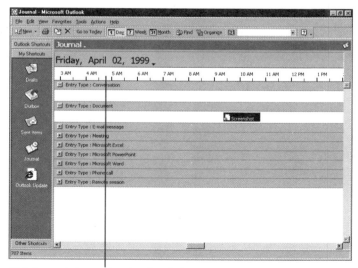

This Journal shows the timeline in hours.

Moving and Removing Journal Entries

As you begin to rely more on the Journal and start using it to organize and track your activities, you may find that some entries end up in the wrong location or are no longer needed. Fortunately, it's easy to both move and remove Journal entries.

TIP

Only entries are deleted. *When you delete a Journal entry, only the entry—and not the item it refers to—is deleted.*

TRY THIS

Nowhere to hide. *To see all of your Journal entries at once (so that you can find and delete Journal entries you do not want to keep), choose Current View from the View menu and Entry List from the submenu.*

Move a Journal Entry

1 Double-click the Journal entry you want to move to some other point on the timeline.

2 Enter a new start date and time and a new end date and time, if necessary.

3 Click the Save And Close toolbar button.

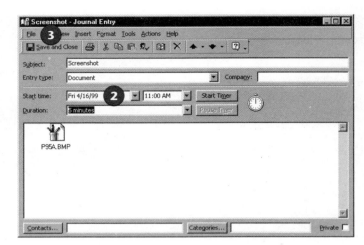

Delete a Journal Entry

1 Select the Journal entry you want to delete.

2 Click the Delete toolbar button.

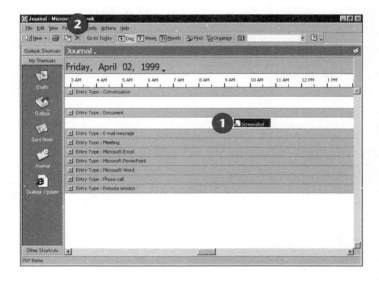

Printing a Journal Entry

For times when you need a hard copy reference, you can print a Journal entry, too. To do this, simply select the Journal entry you want to print. Then choose Print from the File menu, or click the Print toolbar button.

Print a Journal Entry

1. Select the Journal entry you want to print.

2. Choose Print from the File menu.

3. Select the printer you want to use from the Name drop-down list box.

4. Specify how many copies you want to print in the Number Of Copies box.

5. Click OK.

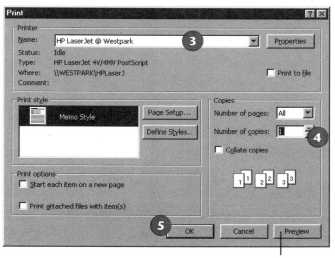

Click to see what the printed Journal entry will look like.

Using Notes

Many people find their desks littered with little yellow sticky notes. They can be used in so many different ways: as reminder notes, for telephone numbers, and for the names and addresses of people to write or call or contact in some way.

The funny thing is, it's handy to use notes on your computer's desktop, too—and in all the same ways: for reminder notes, telephone numbers, and other bits of trivia. For this reason, Microsoft Outlook includes a simple Notes feature. The step-by-step instructions in this section will help you get the knack of Outlook's Notes quickly.

Creating Notes

You create note items in much the same way that you create any word processing document or text file. Once you've created a note item, you display the item in the same way that you display other Outlook items.

TIP

Drag-and-drop creation.
You can create a note out of any other type of Outlook item by dragging the item onto the Notes icon on the Outlook Bar. This creates a new note with the information from the item you selected.

Create a Note

1 Display your Notes folder.

2 Click the New toolbar button.

3 Type the note text in the note window.

4 Click the Close button to have Outlook automatically save the note.

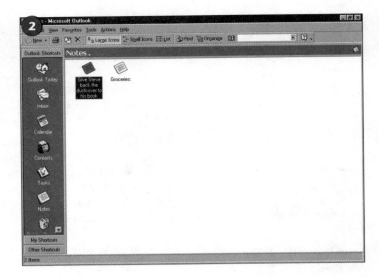

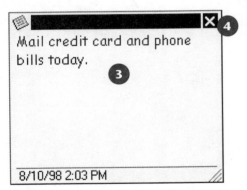

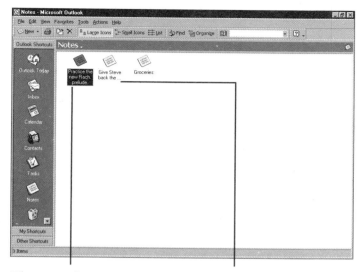

TIP

Copy note text by dragging. *You can copy text between note windows by dragging. To do this, open both the first note with the text you want to copy and the second note in which you want to copy the text. Select the text you want to copy from the first note, and then while holding down the Ctrl key, drag it to the second note.*

TIP

Restore a vanished note. *If the first note disappears when you open the second note, you can restore the first note by clicking its button on the Windows Taskbar.*

Display a Note

1 Display your Notes folder.

2 Double-click the note icon for the note you want to read.

When you select a note, Outlook displays the first paragraph.

Outlook displays the first few words of the note beneath the note icon.

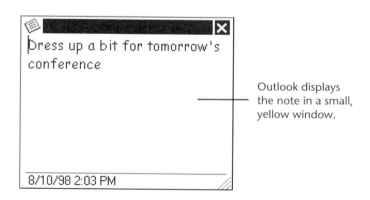

Outlook displays the note in a small, yellow window.

10

Editing Notes

You can easily make changes to the notes you create with Outlook. You simply open the Notes folder, double-click the note item to open it, and then make your changes.

Edit a Note's Text

1. Display the note you want to edit.

2. To replace text: select the text you want to replace by dragging the mouse over the text; then type the replacement text.

3. To insert new text: click to place the cursor where you want new text; then type the text.

Move Text Within a Note

1. Select the text you want to move.

2. Drag the text to the new location.

Click the text selection, and then drag it to the new location.

Copy Text Within a Note

1. Select the text you want to copy.

2. Click the text selection, and then while holding down the Ctrl key, drag it to the new location.

Cleaning Up the Notes Folder

You work with note items and the Notes folder in much the same way that you work with other Outlook folders and items.

Delete a Note You've Just Displayed

1. Click the Control menu icon on the note window.

2. Choose Delete from the shortcut menu.

Delete a Note in the Notes Folder

1. Select the note you want to delete.

2. Click the Delete toolbar button.

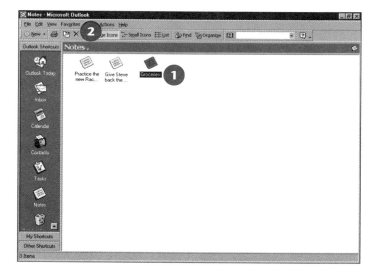

TIP

Outlook deletes instantly. *Outlook doesn't provide a confirmation message box when you choose the Delete command, so be careful that you don't accidentally delete notes. If you do accidentally delete a note, you can restore it from the Deleted Items folder.*

TIP

Use the Delete key. *You can quickly delete any Outlook item by selecting the item and pressing the Delete, or Del, key on your keyboard.*

10

Working with Note Windows

You create, edit, print, and save notes in much the same way that you create, edit, print, and save word processing documents. If you're familiar with any word processor or text editor, you'll have no trouble learning how to work with notes.

TIP

Change defaults. *You can change your note color, size, and font default settings by choosing Options from the Tools menu. Click the Preferences tab, and then click Note Options. Use the Note Options dialog box to change the default settings for all your notes.*

TIP

Move notes. *To move a note window to a new location, drag the note window's title bar.*

Recolor a Note Window

1. Display your Notes folder.

2. Double-click the note icon for the note you want to recolor.

3. Click the Control menu icon on the note window.

4. Choose Color from the shortcut menu.

5. Choose a color for the note window from the submenu.

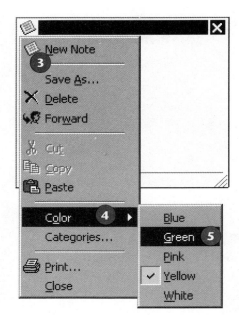

Resize a Note Window

1. Click the lower right corner of the window and drag.

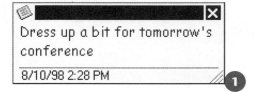

Customizing the Notes Folder

Once you've created a few notes and feel comfortable working in the Notes folder, you may want to customize the Notes Folder view to make it more efficient for you.

SEE ALSO

See "Sorting Items" on page 168 for information on sorting Outlook's folders.

TIP

Icon placement options.
To be able to move your notes wherever you want, click the Do Not Arrange option button. To keep your notes lined up in a grid as you move them, click the Line Up Icons option button. To line up your notes in rows, click the AutoArrange option button. To line up your notes in rows and sort them by the criteria you specify, click the Sort And AutoArrange option button.

Change the Notes Folder View

1. Display your Notes folder.

2. Click the Large Icons, Small Icons, or List toolbar buttons to change the way Outlook displays your notes in the Notes folder.

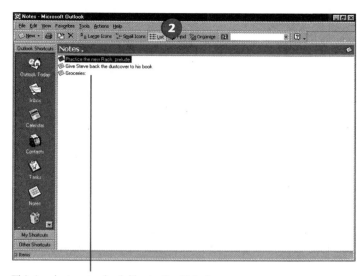

This is what notes look like in the List view.

Customize the Note Icon Placement

1. Choose Current View from the View menu and Customize Current View from the submenu.

2. Click Other Settings.

3. Click an Icon Placement option button to tell Outlook how you want to organize your note icons.

4. Click OK.

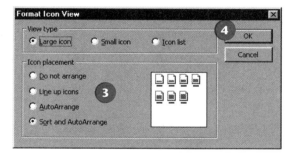

10

Sharing Notes

Notes aren't an ideal tool to use for sharing information —just as those yellow sticky notes they mimic aren't. Nevertheless, you can share the information you enter in note windows in a variety of ways. You can print a note's text and then distribute the printed note. You can save a note's text in a file that can be opened by other applications (such as your word processor). And you can even e-mail notes to other Outlook users.

TIP

Print preview. *To see how your note will print without actually printing it, click Preview in the Print dialog box.*

TIP

Use a note in a word processor. *If you want to use a note's text in a word processing program, save the note in either the text (*.txt) or Rich Text Format (*.rtf) file formats.*

Print a Note

1. Select the note you want to print.

2. Click the Print toolbar button.

3. Click OK.

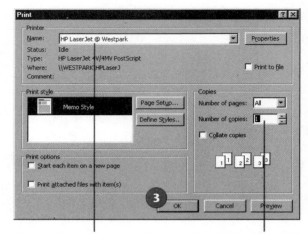

Use the Name box to specify which printer you want to use.

Use the Number Of Copies box to specify how many copies of the note you want printed.

Save a Note to a Text File

1. Click the Control menu icon in the note window.

2. Choose Save As from the shortcut menu.

3. Specify where you want the text file saved in the Save In drop-down list box.

4. Type a new name for the file in the File Name text box.

5. Click Save.

Specify the file format you want the new file to use in the Save As Type drop-down list box, if necessary.

Sharing notes with people who don't use Outlook. *In order for someone to see your note as a note, they need to also use the Outlook personal information manager. If your recipients use another e-mail program, you'll want to copy your note text to the Message window. To copy note text to the window, display the note with the text you want to share, open a Message window, select the text you want to copy, and then hold down the Ctrl key and drag the text from the note window to the Message window.*

Use your keyboard to copy and paste. *Select the text you'd like to copy, and then while holding down the Ctrl key, press the C key to copy it or the X key to cut it. Place the cursor where you'd like to insert the text, and then hold down the Ctrl key and press the V key.*

Notes become tasks. *If you want to create a task or a task request from a note, drag the note from the Notes folder to the Tasks icon on the Outlook Bar.*

Forward a Note as Part of an E-Mail Message

1. Right-click the note icon for the note you want to forward.

2. Choose Forward from the shortcut menu.

3. Type the recipient's name in the To text box.

4. Optionally, type the names of the recipients of courtesy copies in the Cc text box.

5. Describe the purpose or subject of the e-mail message in the Subject text box.

6. Optionally, add any text you want to accompany the note.

7. Click the Send toolbar button.

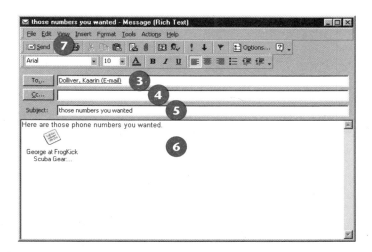

10

Using Outlook as a Desktop Manager

In addition to accomplishing the many different tasks described in the preceding sections, Microsoft Outlook can also manage the files and folders on your disk. With Outlook, you can locate and open files on your computer. You can also create new folders and copy or move files between folders, disks, or even computers on a network. You can even save Outlook items as files on your computer. In fact, the more you use Outlook, the more you will realize that you may be able to do all your housekeeping with this one versatile tool.

Viewing Files and File Properties

Almost everything you do in Microsoft Office is saved as a file. Often these files are stored in folders so that you can group documents that belong together. For example, you might want all of your letters, interview materials, and drafts of your resumé to be placed in a folder named Job Search. Likewise, as you accumulate more items in Outlook, you will want to be able to create new folders and organize your Outlook items in a way that fits your needs.

TIP

View the Folder list. *To make Outlook work more like Windows Explorer so that you can easily copy and move files by dragging, display the Folder list. To do this, choose Folder List from the View menu.*

Show the Contents of My Computer

1. Click the Other Shortcuts button on the Outlook Bar.

2. Click the My Computer icon.

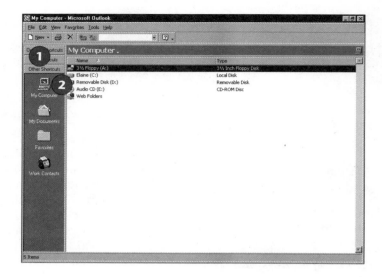

TIP

Can't find a file? *If you cannot see the file you want, you might have to double-click the folder in which it is contained.*

TIP

Use the Web toolbar. *You can use the Web toolbar to navigate your folders. To turn on the Web toolbar, choose Toolbars from the View menu and click Web.*

TIP

Click the question mark. *If you have a question about one of the Properties dialog box's buttons or boxes, click the dialog box's Help (question mark) button and then click the item you have a question about.*

Open a File in My Computer

1 Display the contents of My Computer.

2 Double-click the drive that contains the file you want to view.

3 Double-click the file you want to open.

View the Properties of a File

1 Display the contents of My Computer.

2 Double-click the drive that contains the file with the properties you want to view.

3 Right-click the file.

4 Choose Properties from the shortcut menu.

5 Click OK when you've finished viewing the properties.

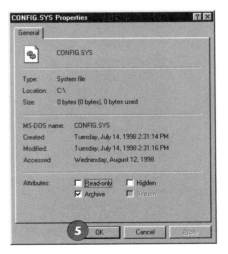

11

Renaming and Copying Files and Folders

Renaming files helps you keep your files current. Copying files lets you take advantage of existing information by incorporating it into new items and documents.

Rename a File or Folder

1 Display the contents of My Computer.

2 Double-click the drive that contains the file or folder you want to rename.

3 Right-click the file or folder you want to rename.

4 Choose Rename from the shortcut menu.

5 Type a new name in the New Name text box.

6 Click OK.

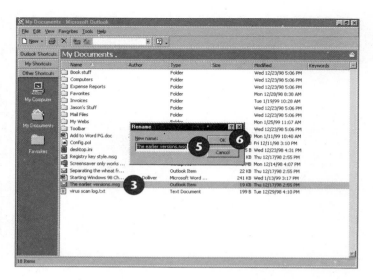

Copy a File or Folder to a Floppy Disk

1 Display the contents of My Computer.

2 Double-click the drive that contains the file or folder you want to copy.

3 Right-click the file or folder you want to copy.

4 Choose Send To from the shortcut menu, and select the drive where you want to copy the file or folder.

Copy and paste files.
*You can copy files to other
locations by right-clicking the
file and choosing Copy from
the shortcut menu. Then right-
click the location where you
want to copy the file, and
choose Paste from the shortcut
menu.*

Copy a floppy. *To copy the
contents of one floppy disk to
another floppy disk, choose
Copy Disk from the File menu.*

Format a Floppy Disk

1. Display the contents of
   My Computer.

2. Select the floppy drive
   with the disk you want
   to format.

3. Insert the disk into the disk
   drive, and choose Format
   from the File menu.

4. Select the capacity of the
   floppy disk you inserted.

5. Select a formatting option.

   ◆ Choose Quick if the
     disk is already format-
     ted and you just want
     to erase its contents.
   ◆ Choose Full if the disk
     is unformatted or is
     formatted for the
     Macintosh.

6. Select the Display Summary When Finished
   check box.

7. Click Start.

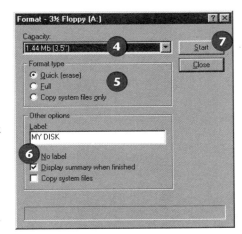

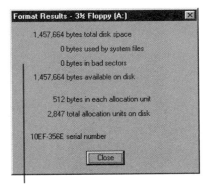

The Summary dialog box tells you
whether the disk has errors.

11

Creating Folders and Shortcuts

There are many ways to move around your Outlook files and folders, but perhaps the fastest way is by creating and using a shortcut to a file or folder.

Create a New Folder

1 Display the contents of My Computer.

2 Double-click the drive on which you want to create the new folder.

3 If necessary, double-click the folder in which you want to create a new subfolder.

4 Choose New from the File menu and Folder from the submenu.

5 Type a name for the new folder in the Name text box.

6 Click OK.

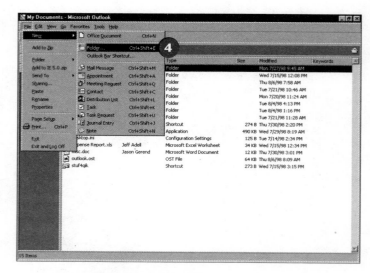

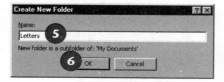

Copy a file or folder. *If you're trying to create a file or folder shortcut and you choose Paste from the Edit menu, you create a new copy of the file or folder rather than a shortcut to the file or folder.*

Move a file or folder. *You can move a file or folder by choosing Cut from the shortcut menu (rather than Copy) and Paste from the Edit menu (rather than Paste Shortcut).*

Create a shortcut. *To create a shortcut to a file or folder on your desktop, choose Send To from the shortcut menu and Desktop As Shortcut from the submenu.*

Create a Shortcut to a File or Folder

1 Display the contents of My Computer.

2 Double-click the drive that contains the file or folder to which you want to create a shortcut.

3 Right-click the file or folder to which you want to create a shortcut.

4 Choose Copy from the shortcut menu.

5 Open the file or folder where you want the shortcut to appear, and choose Paste Shortcut from the Edit menu.

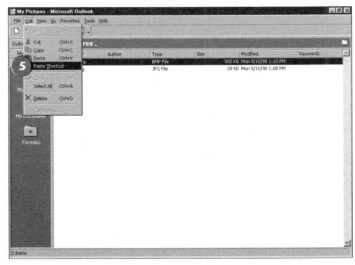

Using Outlook on a Network

More than ever, computers are connected to one another to form networks, because this is the most efficient way to share information. If your computer is part of a network, you will find that much of what you do in Outlook has a network component to it. Before you can share any information from Outlook, however, you must first be connected to a network drive.

TIP

Network drive paths.
When entering a network drive's path, use the form \\computer\drive, in which "computer" is the name of the computer to which you want to map and "drive" is the name of the drive on that computer to which you want to map.

Connect to a Network Drive

1. Display the contents of My Computer.

2. Click the Map Network Drive toolbar button.

3. Enter the network drive's path in the Path box.

4. Click OK.

Share a Folder or Drive

1. Display the contents of My Computer.

2. Right-click the folder or drive you want to share.

3. Choose Sharing from the shortcut menu.

4. Click the Shared As option button.

5. Enter a name for others to use when connecting to the folder or drive.

6. If necessary, select an option to specify access rights to the folder.

7. Click OK.

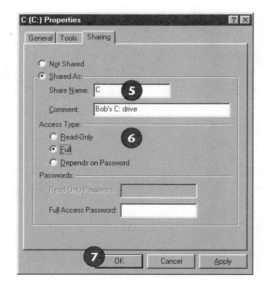

Speed up your logon. *If you disconnect from network drives you don't regularly use, your computer will log on to its network more quickly.*

Disconnect from a Network Drive

1 Display the contents of My Computer.

2 Click the Disconnect Network Drive toolbar button.

3 Select the network drive you want to disconnect.

4 Click OK.

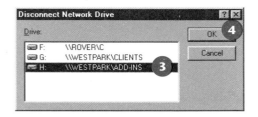

11

Finding Files

As you use your computer more, you'll create more files, and there's always the chance that one will be misplaced. Outlook offers several tools to help you find files or folders you can't locate. Remember, too, that you can also use the Find command on the Microsoft Windows Start menu to find files and folders.

TIP

Wildcards. *If you know only part of the name of the file, enter what you know and use the asterisk (*) as a wildcard to stand for the parts you don't know.*

TIP

Use Advanced Find. *Advanced Find is not available on the Tools menu when displaying My Computer. Click the Outlook Today toolbar button, and then choose Advanced Find from the Tools menu.*

Find a File

1 Right-click the drive or folder you want to search, and choose Find from the shortcut menu.

2 Select the Files entry from the Look For drop-down list box.

3 If you know the name of the file you're looking for, enter it in the Named text box.

4 Select the type of file you're looking for in the Of Type drop-down list box.

5 Click Find Now.

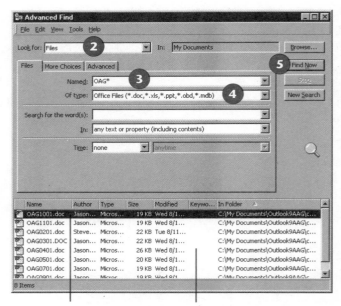

Double-click an item to open it.

Items that match your search criteria are listed at the bottom of the Find window.

Working with Items

Items—whether appointments or Journal entries—can be saved as files. Saving items as files allows you and others to work with the items using other applications.

TRY THIS

List box tricks. *You can right-click a file or folder shown in the list box beneath the Save In drop-down list box to display a handy shortcut menu of file and folder commands.*

TIP

Use the Places Bar. *Use the buttons on the Places Bar to quickly access folders or files you frequently use.*

Save an Item as a File

1. Click the item you want to save.

2. Choose Save As from the File menu.

3. Type a name for the file in the File Name text box.

4. Select the file type you want from the Save As Type drop-down list box.

5. Specify where you want to save the file in the Save In drop-down list box.

6. Click Save.

12

Customizing Outlook

Because Microsoft Outlook is really a personal information manager, it provides you with a great deal of flexibility in deciding how to present and organize the information stored in its folders. This flexibility allows you to organize your information in whatever ways make most sense to you. Specifically, Outlook lets you customize the program in four different ways:

◆ You can create rules, categorize items, use different views, and even create your own views to specify, organize, and arrange the item information that Outlook displays in the Information Viewer.

◆ You can customize the Outlook application window so that it looks and works the way you want by adding, removing, and customizing toolbars and the Outlook Bar.

◆ You can choose Options from the Tools menu to change the way Outlook actually operates, such as specifying when items are spell-checked, how messages get delivered, and how Outlook archives old items.

◆ You can add and edit profiles and services to Outlook to specify where, when, and how you want to connect to information services.

This final section of *Microsoft Outlook 2000 At a Glance* describes many of the changes you can make, paying particular attention to those options that are most likely to interest new users of Outlook.

Creating Rules to Automatically Move Items

Using Outlook's Organize pane, you can organize the items in your folders. For example, you can tell Outlook to move all the items sent to or received from a particular contact to a separate folder.

TRY THIS

Select an item first. *Instead of entering the contact's name in the text box, select an item sent to or received from the contact. Outlook enters the contact's name for you.*

TIP

Close the Organize pane. *Click the Organize pane's Close button to stop displaying the Organize pane in a folder.*

TIP

Create advanced rules. *Use the Rules Wizard to create rules to notify you of incoming messages, flag specific messages, assign categories to messages, or automatically check for new messages.*

Move All Items to or from a Contact to Another Folder

1. Open the folder from which you want Outlook to automatically move items to another folder.

2. Click the Organize toolbar button.

3. Click the Using Folders tab.

4. Specify whether you want to move items sent to or received from a specific contact.

5. In the From or To text box, enter the name of the contact.

6. In the last drop-down list box, select the folder to which you want the items moved.

7. Click Create.

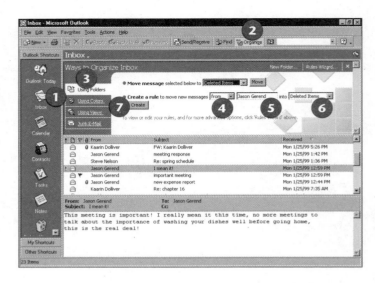

Identifying Messages by Color

You can also use the Organize pane to create rules to color-code messages that you send to or receive from particular contacts.

> **TIP**
>
> **Different tabs.** *Which tabs you have available in the Organize pane depends on the folder you're organizing.*

> **TIP**
>
> **Create out-of-office rules.** *To automatically handle messages when you are out of the office, choose Out Of Office Assistant from the Tools menu. Use the Out Of Office Assistant dialog box to compose the text of your AutoReply message. Then click Add Rule to specify which messages you want Outlook to automatically handle and what you want Outlook to do with the messages (to reply to them or forward them to someone else, for example). Note: This feature is only available for use with Microsoft Exchange Server.*

Color-Code Messages

1 Open the folder with the messages you want to color-code.

2 Click the Organize toolbar button.

3 Click the Using Colors tab.

4 Specify whether you want to color mesages sent to or received from a specific contact.

5 In the From or To text box, enter the name of the contact.

6 In the last drop-down list box, select the color you want Outlook to use to code the messages.

7 Click Apply Color.

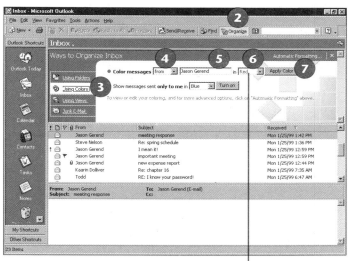

Select a color from the drop-down list box, and click Turn On to have Outlook color messages with your name in the To box.

Using Different Views

You can change a folder's view to change the information Outlook displays and the way in which it displays the information.

Change the Current View

1. Display the folder with the view you want to change.

2. Click the Organize toolbar button.

3. Click the Using Views tab.

4. Select a new view from the list box.

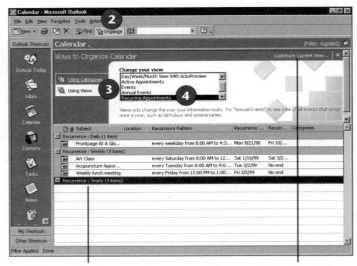

This view shows recurring appointments entered in the Calendar.

Click Customize Current View to customize the view you select.

Handling Junk Mail

Electronic mail is sometimes very similar to regular mail—the longer you live at an address and the more you correspond, the more unwanted commercial mail you receive. Luckily, with Outlook 2000, you can automatically separate junk mail from the personal mail you want to read.

TIP

Create a Junk E-Mail folder.
If you tell Outlook to move junk mail to the Junk E-Mail folder and you have not yet created this folder, Outlook asks whether you want to create the folder. Click Yes to have Outlook create a Junk E-Mail folder for you.

TIP

Add people to junk lists.
To add a person to your Junk Senders or Adult Content Senders lists, right-click a message received from the sender and choose Junk E-Mail from the shortcut menu. Then choose Add To Junk Senders List or Add To Adult Content Senders List from the submenu.

Handle Junk Mail

1. Display your Inbox.

2. Click the Organize toolbar button.

3. Click the Junk E-Mail tab.

4. To move or color mail sent to you by someone on your Junk Senders list, specify whether you want the mail moved or colored. Then specify a new location or color. Click Turn On.

5. To move or color mail with adult content, specify whether you want the mail moved or colored. Then specify a new location or color. Click Turn On.

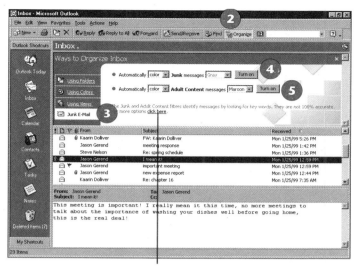

Click this button to view the list of names on your Junk Senders list or to add a new name to the list.

Working with Categories

A category is a word or phrase that helps you organize information so that it can be used more efficiently and found more easily. For example, you might want to create a category for business contacts and one for personal contacts or a category for weekday tasks and one for weekend tasks. Outlook comes with a preestablished selection of categories, but you can add as many as you want of your own also.

TIP

Use Categories in other folders. *You can also work with categories in the Calendar, Contacts, Tasks, and Journal folders by clicking the Organize toolbar button.*

TIP

All Outlook items. *The categories you create can be used with all Outlook items.*

TIP

No folders or files. *You can categorize Outlook items, but you can't categorize folders or files.*

Create a Category

1. Select an Outlook item.

2. Choose Categories from the Edit menu.

3. Click Master Category List.

4. Type a name for the category in the New Category text box.

5. Click Add.

6. Click OK, and then click OK again.

Assign an Item to a Category

1. Select the item you want to assign to a category.

2. Choose Categories from the Edit menu.

3. Select the check boxes in the Available Categories list box next to the categories to which you want to assign the item.

4. Click OK.

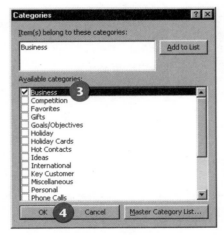

Remove an Item from a Category

1. Select the item you want to remove from a category.

2. Choose Categories from the Edit menu.

3. Click to clear the check boxes for the categories from which you want the item removed.

4. Click OK.

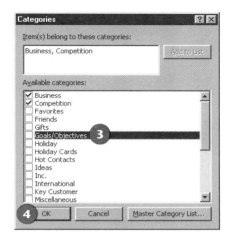

TIP

Remove a category completely. *If you delete a category from the Master List, items that have already been assigned to that category will still be assigned to it. To remove the category completely from the Available Categories list box, you need to delete the category for all the specific items that you have assigned to it.*

Delete a Category

1. Select an Outlook item.

2. Choose Categories from the Edit menu.

3. Click Master Category List.

4. Click the category or categories you want to delete.

5. Click Delete.

6. Click OK.

12

Customizing Views

Views allow you to look at the same information from a different perspective. They also allow you to control the amount of information that is revealed. You can customize views of folders to show just the information you want by specifying which fields appear.

TIP

Control field order. *If you want to change the order in which fields appear in the view, click Move Up or Move Down. The first field shown in the Show These Fields In This Order list box appears in the leftmost column of a view.*

Choose Which Fields Appear

1. Display the folder and the view you want to customize.

2. Choose Current View from the View menu and Customize Current View from the submenu.

3. Click Fields.

4. Double-click the fields in the Available Fields list box that you want to appear in the Folder view.

5. Double-click the fields in the Show These Fields In This Order list box that you don't want to appear in the Folder view.

6. Click OK.

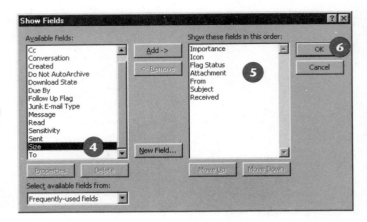

Grouping Items

You can group Outlook items together so that they appear in a subfolder. For example, you could group contact items by company names, thereby grouping contacts by company. Or you could group message items by priority, thereby segregating your most important messages from all the others.

TIP

Different fields for different types. *Which fields you can use to group items depends on the type of item.*

TRY THIS

Regroup. *To remove the grouping fields you've set using the Group By dialog box, click Clear All.*

Group Folder Items

1. Display the folder that contains the items you want to group.

2. Choose Current View from the View menu and Customize Current View from the submenu.

3. Click Group By.

4. Select the first grouping field from the Group Items By drop-down list box.

5. Click either the Ascending or Descending option button.

6. Optionally, to group items within groups, select entries from the Then By drop-down list boxes.

7. Click OK.

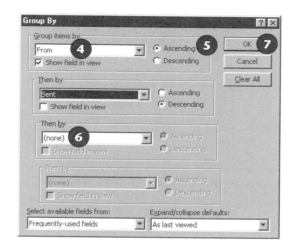

Sorting Items

You can order, or sort, the items in an Outlook folder using item information, or fields. For example, you can sort message items alphabetically by the sender's name. You can also sort task items by due date.

Sort Folder Items

1. Display the folder containing the items you want to sort.

2. Choose Current View from the View menu and Customize Current View from the submenu.

3. Click Sort.

4. Select your first sort field from the Sort Items By drop-down list box.

5. Click either the Ascending or Descending option button.

6. Optionally, to sort items with the same primary key, select entries from the Then By drop-down list boxes.

7. Click OK.

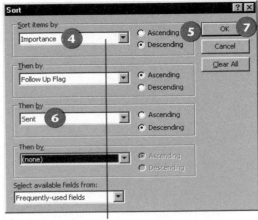

What you specify in the Sort Items By drop-down list box becomes your primary sort key.

Formatting a View

You can customize both the existing views that Outlook supplies and the new views you create from scratch.

Format a View

1. Display the folder and the view you want to customize.

2. Choose Current View from the View menu and Customize Current View from the submenu.

3. Click Other Settings.

4. Click a Font button to display a dialog box in which you can specify the font, font style, and font size.

5. If you're formatting a table-style view, specify whether you want to display this view's items in a grid, and if so, what the grid should look like.

6. Click OK.

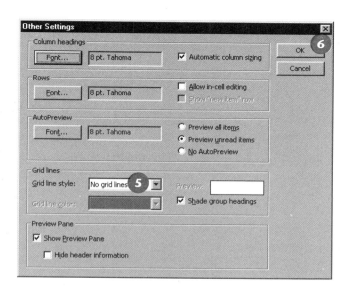

Using Filters

You can use a filter to view only the items that meet conditions you have predefined. For example, a filter would work well if you want to view only high-priority items or only those items you've categorized as business-related.

TIP

Different options and tabs. *Outlook provides different filtering options for different folders. Note, too, that the name of the first tab in the Filter dialog box changes depending on the type of item you're filtering.*

TRY THIS

Search by item creation dates and times. *If you know when an item was created (in the case of messages, contacts, and notes) or when an item is supposed to start or finish (in the case of tasks and appointments), you can use this information as part of your search criteria. Select the time information that you know from the first Time drop-down list box. Then select a date or time from the second Time drop-down list box.*

Filter Items Based on Content

1 Display the folder that contains the items you want to filter.

2 Choose Current View from the View menu and Customize Current View from the submenu.

3 Click Filter.

4 Click the leftmost tab (in this case, the Appointments And Meetings tab).

5 If you want to show only those items that include a word or phrase, use the Search For The Word(s) text box to specify that word or phrase.

6 If you use the Search For The Word(s) text box to specify search criteria, select an entry from the In drop-down list box to specify where Outlook should look when it examines folder items.

7 Click OK.

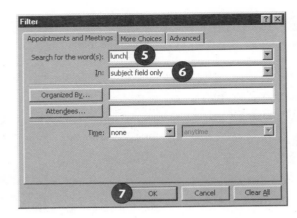

Filter Items Based on Category

1. Display the folder that contains the items you want to filter.

2. Choose Current View from the View menu and Customize Current View from the submenu.

3. Click Filter.

4. Click the More Choices tab.

5. Click Categories.

6. Identify the categories you want to use to filter items by selecting check boxes in the Available Categories list box.

7. Click OK.

8. Click OK.

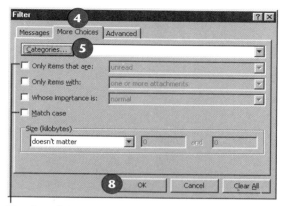

Use these boxes to apply additional filter criteria.

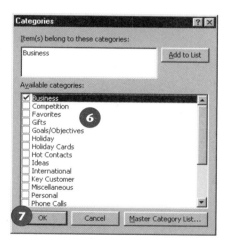

Creating a New Folder View

You can create entirely new views if none of Outlook's existing views works the way you want.

TIP

Where new views appear.
When you create a new view, it is added to the View menu's Current View submenu.

Create a New View

1. Display the folder for which you want to create a view.

2. Choose Current View from the View menu and Define Views from the submenu.

3. Click New.

4. Type the name of the new view in the Name Of New View text box.

5. Select the general appearance, or organization, of the view from the Type Of View list box.

6. Click one of the Can Be Used On option buttons to describe how this view will be available.

7. Click OK.

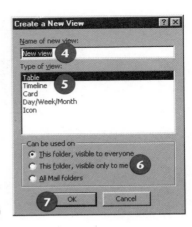

New views work the same.
Grouping, sorting, filtering, and formatting the items in a new view works exactly like grouping, sorting, filtering, and formatting items in an existing view.

8 Click Fields; then use the Show Fields dialog box to describe what pieces of information you want presented in the view.

9 Click Group By; then use the Group By dialog box to describe how you want items grouped in the view.

10 Click Sort; then use the Sort dialog box to describe how you want items ordered in the view.

11 Click Filter; then use the Filter dialog box to describe which items you want included and excluded from the view.

12 Click Other Settings; then use the Other Settings dialog box to describe how you want the items to look in the view.

13 Click OK to return to the Define Views dialog box.

14 Click Apply View to display the folder's items using the new view.

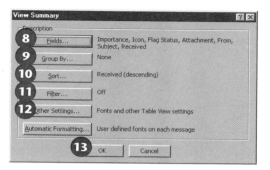

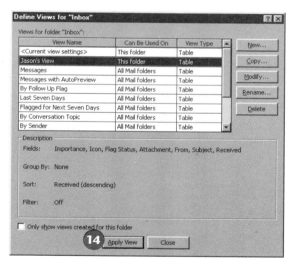

Customizing the Outlook Program Window

The status bar appears at the bottom of the Outlook window and describes how many items are in a folder. The Outlook Bar appears along the left edge of the Outlook window and provides clickable icons. You'll typically want to use the status bar and the Outlook Bar, but you don't have to. You can remove them, and add them back later.

> **TIP**
>
> **When the status bar is displayed.** *If you are currently displaying the status bar, Outlook places a check mark next to Status Bar on the Tools menu.*

> **TIP**
>
> **Add the Folder list.** *If you remove the Outlook Bar, you'll probably want to add the Folder list since it provides another easy way to display the items in an Outlook folder.*

Add and Remove the Status Bar

1. Display an Outlook folder.

2. Choose Status Bar from the View menu.

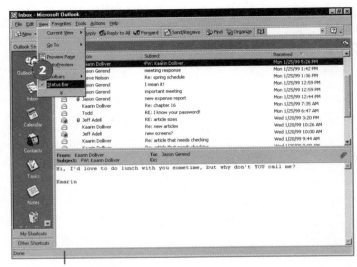

This is the status bar.

Add and Remove the Outlook Bar

1. Display an Outlook folder.

2. Choose Outlook Bar from the View menu.

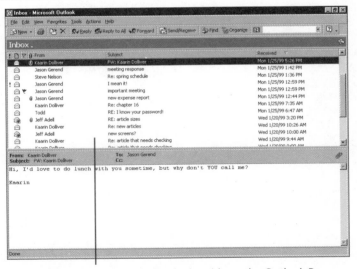

This is how the Outlook window looks without the Outlook Bar.

Choosing Which Toolbars Appear

One of the easiest changes you can make to your Outlook window is to include or exclude toolbars. You can choose which toolbars appear and which don't.

TIP

Available Toolbars. *Which toolbars you can add to the Outlook window depends on what information appears in the Information Viewer or the active window.*

TIP

Active toolbars. *If a toolbar appears in the Outlook window, Outlook places a check mark next to its Toolbars submenu command.*

TIP

Missing buttons. *If you think some of the buttons are missing on a toolbar, maximize the window to see all the buttons.*

Add and Remove a Toolbar

1 Choose Toolbars from the View menu.

2 Choose the submenu command that corresponds to the toolbar you want to add.

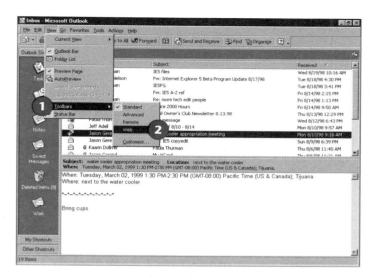

12

Customizing the Outlook Bar

In addition to choosing whether to display or hide the Outlook Bar, you can also customize the Outlook Bar to make it more efficient for you. You can add new shortcut icons and you can create new groups of shortcuts.

> **TRY THIS**
>
> **Need more room?** *To fit more icons on the Outlook Bar, right-click the Outlook Bar and choose Small Icons from the shortcut menu.*

Add a Shortcut to the Outlook Bar

1. Right-click the Outlook Bar.

2. Choose Outlook Bar Shortcut from the shortcut menu.

3. Use the Look In drop-down list box to specify whether the shortcut is to an Outlook folder or a folder on your computer.

4. Use the list box to specify the folder you want to add to the Outlook Bar.

5. Click OK.

Rename groups. *To rename an existing group, right-click the button of the group you want to rename and choose Rename Group from the shortcut menu.*

Delete a group. *To delete a group, right-click the button of the group you want to delete and choose Remove Group from the shortcut menu.*

Add a New Group to the Outlook Bar

1 Right-click the Outlook Bar.

2 Choose Add New Group from the shortcut menu. Outlook adds a new button to the Outlook Bar.

3 Enter a name for the new group, and press the Enter key.

4 Add new shortcuts to the new group or move existing shortcuts from other groups to the new group by dragging them to the group's label.

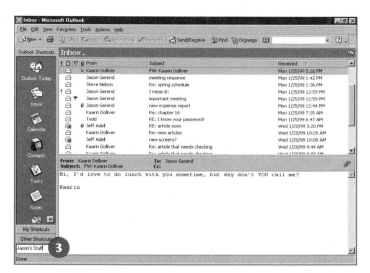

12

Customizing Toolbars and Menus

Outlook's Personalized Toolbars And Menus feature automatically customizes toolbars and menus based on the commands you frequently use. But if you find that you want to change the buttons on toolbars, Outlook makes it easy to customize toolbars yourself. You can also tell Outlook not to customize your menus.

TIP

Rearrange buttons. *To rearrange buttons on a new or existing toolbar, hold down the Alt key and then drag the desired button to a new location.*

Add a Custom Toolbar

1. Choose Toolbars from the View menu and Customize from the submenu.

2. Click New.

3. Enter a name for the new toolbar in the dialog box Outlook provides, and click OK.

4. Click the Commands tab.

5. Select a menu name from the list to display the list of commands on that menu.

6. Select a command from the list.

7. Drag the command to the new toolbar.

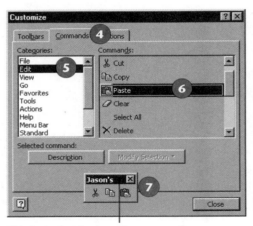

This is the beginning of a new toolbar.

Add to existing toolbars.
*To add new buttons to an
existing toolbar, select a
command name from the list
on the Commands tab and
drag it to any toolbar you have
displayed on your screen.*

**Outlook customizes
menus for you.** *Outlook puts
commands you frequently use
at the top of menus and takes
little-used commands and
hides them. To see hidden
commands, click the arrows at
the bottom of a menu.*

8 Click the Options tab.

9 Select the check boxes to
specify how you want the
new toolbar to look.

10 Click Close.

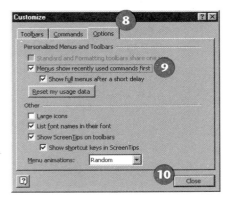

Turn Off Personalized Menus

1 Choose Toolbars from the
View menu and Custom-
ize from the submenu.

2 Click the Options tab.

3 Clear the Menus check
box to show recently used
commands first.

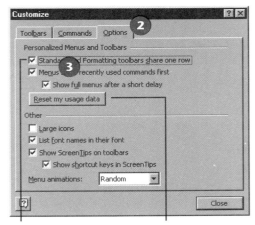

Select this check box with
a new message open to
make the Standard and
Formatting toolbars appear
in one row.

Press here to reset
your usage data for
menu and toolbar
commands.

12

Setting Outlook's General Options

With the Tools menu's Options command, Outlook gives you control over just about every facet of its operation. The Other tab lets you make changes in the overall operation of Outlook.

TIP

Your Outlook may vary.
The tabs and options you have available in the Options dialog box depend on how you installed Outlook.

Tell Outlook to Empty the Deleted Items Folder Each Time You Exit

1 Choose Options from the Tools menu.

2 Click the Other tab.

3 Select the Empty The Deleted Items Folder Upon Exiting check box if you want the items you've sent to the Deleted Items folder permanently deleted when you close Outlook.

4 Click OK.

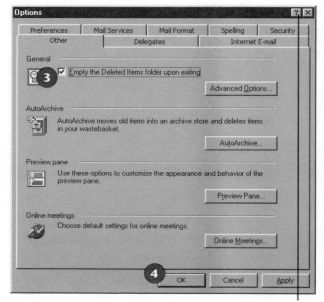

If you have questions about the other settings, click the dialog box's Help (question mark) button and then click a text box, check box, or option button.

Setting AutoArchive Options

The longer you use Outlook, the more items you accumulate in your Outlook folders. To keep old items from cluttering your folders, you can have Outlook archive them with AutoArchive.

TIP

Set AutoArchive properties for individual e-mail folders. *Right-click the e-mail folder and choose Properties from the shortcut menu. Click the AutoArchive tab and set the options you want. Click OK to save and close.*

Tell Outlook When and What to Archive

1. Choose Options from the Tools menu.

2. Click the Other tab.

3. Click AutoArchive.

4. Select the AutoArchive Every check box to turn on the AutoArchive feature.

5. Specify how often Outlook should archive old items.

6. Select the Prompt Before AutoArchive check box to have Outlook alert you that it is time to archive and request confirmation before archiving.

7. Select the Delete Expired Items When AutoArchiving check box to tell Outlook that you don't want to keep expired messages.

8. Click OK.

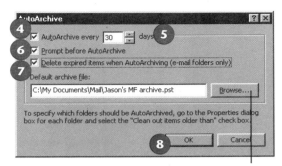

Click Browse to specify a different file for storing archived items.

12

Specifying Preview Pane Options

You can customize the Preview pane so that it looks and works the way you want it to.

TIP

Page down with the Spacebar. *Select the Single Key Reading Using Space Bar check box to be able to use the Spacebar to page down in messages displayed in the Preview pane.*

Describe How the Preview Pane Works

1 Choose Options from the Tools menu.

2 Click the Other tab.

3 Click Preview Pane.

4 Select the Mark Messages As Read In Preview Window check box to have Outlook change a message's status from unread to read when you display it in the Preview pane for a certain length of time.

5 Enter the amount of time you want to be able to display a message in the Preview pane before Outlook marks it as read.

6 Click Font to change the font of messages displayed in the Preview pane.

7 Click OK.

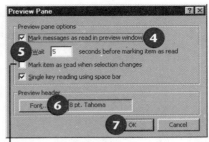

Select this check box if you want Outlook to mark messages viewed in the Preview pane as read only when you move to the next message, not after you've displayed a message for a certain length of time.

Setting Outlook's Advanced Options

The General tab's Advanced Options let you control some of Outlook's more advanced features, such as how Outlook selects text and what font it uses for the Date Navigators.

TIP

Use the Add-In Manager. *Clicking Add-In Manager displays a dialog box that allows you to install or remove the extensions you need for the services you use.*

TIP

Exchange forms. *Clicking Custom Forms displays a dialog box that allows you to specify the storage and use of Exchange forms.*

Change the Advanced Options

1. Choose Options from the Tools menu.

2. Click the Other tab.

3. Click Advanced Options.

4. Select the folder you want Outlook to display when you start the program from the Startup In This Folder drop-down list box.

5. Select the Warn Before Permanently Deleting Items check box if you want Outlook to display a message alerting you when you are about to delete items that you cannot later recover.

6. Select the When Selecting Text, Automatically Select Entire Word check box to have Outlook help you quickly select text.

7. Select the Provide Feedback With Sound check box to use sound Reminders and notification messages.

8. Click OK.

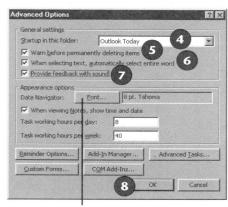

Click this button to change the Date Navigator's font.

12

Specifying How Reminders Work

The Reminder Options dialog box lets you specify when and where Reminder messages appear and how they work.

Change the Way Reminders Work

1. Choose Options from the Tools menu.

2. Click the Other tab.

3. Click Advanced Options.

4. Click Reminder Options.

5. Select the Display The Reminder check box to see Reminder messages.

6. Select the Play Reminder Sound check box to hear a sound when a Reminder message is displayed.

7. Click Browse.

8. Select the folder that stores the sound file you want to play from the Look In drop-down list box.

9. Double-click the sound file you want.

10. Click OK.

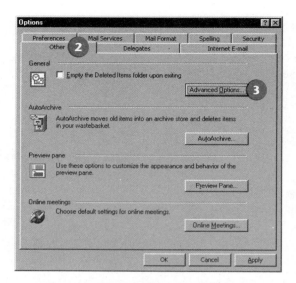

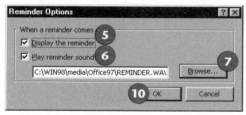

Specifying Message Format

You specify message format to tell Outlook how it should format the messages you send to other people. Outlook allows you to format messages in one of three ways: HTML, Microsoft Outlook Rich Text, and Plain Text

---

TIP

Use Microsoft Word for e-mail. *To use Microsoft Word as your e-mail editor, select the Use Microsoft Word To Edit E-Mail Messages check box.*

TIP

Choose an e-mail format. *Which mail format you should use depends on which e-mail clients the people you usually correspond with have. Depending on their e-mail clients and their Internet service providers, many people will probably not be able to see the formatting you apply. A safe bet is to use the Plain Text format.*

Specify the Message Format

1. Choose Options from the Tools menu.

2. Click the Mail Format tab.

3. Select the format you want to use for writing messages from the Send In This Message Format drop-down list box.

4. If you selected HTML format, you can select a stationery, or background pattern, to use for your outgoing messages.

5. Click Fonts to display a dialog box that you can use to select fonts for composing new messages, replying to and forwarding messages, and reading Plain Text messages.

6. Click OK.

7. Select a default signature to add to all outgoing messages from the Use This Signature By Default drop-down list box.

8. Click OK.

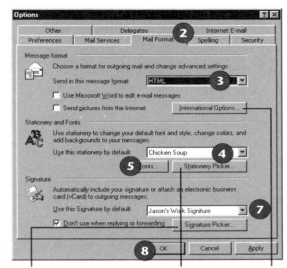

Click this button to add or edit signatures.

Click this button to select your own custom template or stationery.

Click this button to specify character remapping for messages in other languages.

12

Changing the Way Your E-Mail Works

Outlook lets you specify what you want done with your messages under different circumstances.

TIP

Move and delete open items. *To specify what you want Outlook to do after you have moved or deleted an open message, select an entry from the After Moving Or Deleting An Open Item drop-down list box.*

TIP

New mail notification. *To tell Outlook that you want it to display a message box that alerts you when you receive new mail, select the Display A Notification Message When New Mail Arrives check box.*

Specify How Your Inbox Should Work

1 Choose Options from the Tools menu.

2 Click the Preferences tab.

3 Click E-Mail Options.

4 Select the Close Original Message On Reply Or Forward check box to have Outlook close the open Message window when it opens a New Message window for you to compose a reply or forward.

5 Select the Save Copies Of Messages In Sent Items Folder check box to have Outlook automatically save copies of all the messages you send in your Sent Items folder.

6 Select the Automatically Save Unsent Messages check box to have Outlook automatically save messages you're composing to the Drafts folder every three minutes.

7 Click OK.

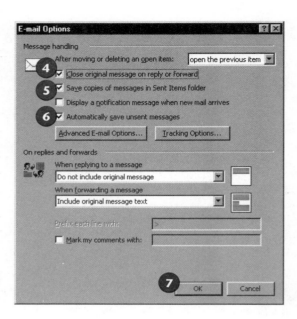

TIP

Set default message importance and sensitivity. *Use the Set Importance and Set Sensitivity drop-down list boxes to set default message importance and sensitivity.*

SEE ALSO

See "Using Outlook's Message-Creation Tools" on page 46 for information on message importance and sensitivity.

Set Advanced E-Mail Options

1 Choose Options from the Tools menu.

2 Click the Preferences tab.

3 Click E-Mail Options.

4 Click Advanced E-Mail Options.

5 Tell Outlook whether and how it should save unsent messages, message replies, and forwarded messages.

6 Describe what Outlook should do to alert you when you receive new mail.

7 Specify whether you want Outlook to automatically process meeting requests and server notification messages.

8 Click OK.

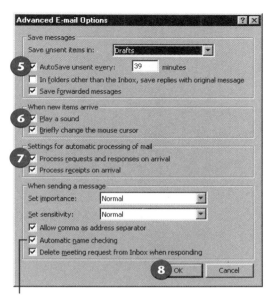

Select this check box to have Outlook automatically check message recipient names against your Address Book list entries.

12

Customizing Internet E-Mail

Use the Internet E-Mail tab of the Options dialog box to specify the format used for sending Internet mail and whether you want Outlook to automatically connect to send and receive Internet mail.

TIP

Uuencode a message.
Click the Uuencode option button to encode messages and attachments in ASCII characters.

Change Your Internet E-Mail Format

1 Choose Options from the Tools menu.

2 Click the Internet E-Mail tab.

3 Click the MIME option button to encode Internet mail and attachments using the Multipurpose Internet Mail Extensions (MIME) protocol. This is the standard format for Internet mail.

4 Click OK.

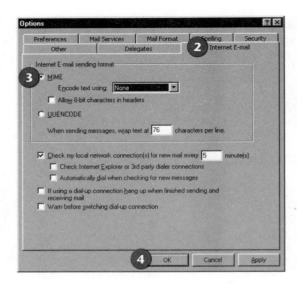

Multiple e-mail services.
*If you have more than one
Internet mail service, select the
Warn Before Switching Dial-
Up Connection check box to
have Outlook warn you before
it disconnects you from one
service in order to dial another
service.*

Customize Your Internet Mail Connection

1 Choose Options from the Tools menu.

2 Click the Internet E-Mail tab.

3 Select the Check My Local Network Connection(s) For New Mail check box to have Outlook automatically look for new Internet mail.

4 Enter how often you want Outlook to look for new Internet mail.

5 Select the Check Internet Explorer or 3rd Party Dialer Connections check box to have Outlook check these services for new Internet mail.

6 Select the Automatically Dial When Checking For New Messages check box to have Outlook automatically dial your Internet service provider.

7 Select the If Using A Dial-Up Connection Hang Up When Finished Sending And Receiving Mail check box if you want Outlook to automatically and immediately disconnect you from the Internet after you've delivered your messages.

8 Click OK.

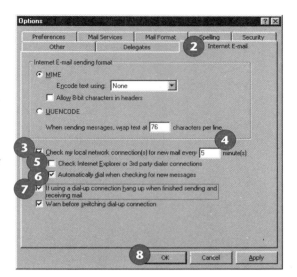

Adding Delegates

If you work on a Exchange Server network, you can grant permission for others on the network to access your Outlook folders and to send items on your behalf.

TIP

Remove a delegate.
To remove a delegate, select the delegate from the list and click Remove.

TIP

Edit permissions. *To edit the permissions for a delegate, select the delegate's name and click Permissions.*

TIP

When you're a delegate.
If someone else has granted you delegate permissions for an Outlook folder, you can view that person's folder by choosing Open from the File menu and Other User's Folder from the submenu. Then enter the person's name in the Name box, select the folder you want to view from the Folder drop-down list box, and click OK.

Add a Delegate

1. Choose Options from the Tools menu.

2. Click the Delegates tab.

3. Click Add.

4. In the Add Users dialog box, double-click the name of the person to whom you want to grant delegate permission.

5. Click OK.

6. Click Permissions, and designate permissions for each of your Exchange folders.

7. Click OK.

8. Click OK.

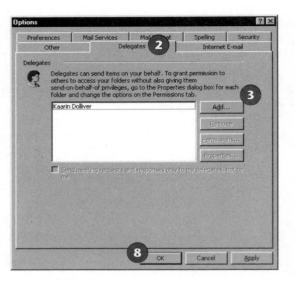

Controlling Spell-Checking

The Spelling tab of the Options dialog box lets you specify how Outlook's built-in spell-checker should work.

TIP

Edit your custom dictionary. *Click Edit to open your custom dictionary in Notepad. You can then add or delete words from your custom dictionary that Outlook checks when it can't find a word in its internal dictionary.*

Change the Way Spell-Checking Works

1. Choose Options from the Tools menu.

2. Click the Spelling tab.

3. Select General Options check boxes to tell Outlook how to check the spelling of your e-mail messages.

4. Click OK.

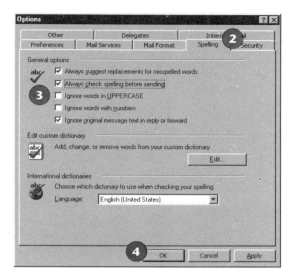

Setting Security Options

Outlook allows you to secure the e-mail you send and to set security options for different sources of Internet material.

> **TIP**
>
> **Digital IDs are set up for you.** *You probably won't need or want to change your digital security settings. When you acquire a digital ID, these settings are installed for you. To view or edit these settings, however, click Change Settings.*

> **TIP**
>
> **Copy digital IDs.** *Click Import/Export Digital ID to copy a digital ID between two computers (for instance, between your laptop and desktop computer).*

> **TIP**
>
> **Get a digital ID.** *Click Get A Digital ID to purchase a digital ID.*

Set Message Security

1. Choose Options from the Tools menu.

2. Click the Security tab.

3. Select an entry from the Default Security Setting drop-down list box to select the digital ID and encryption settings you want to use by default if you have more than one security service.

4. Select the security zone you want to apply for opening HTML messages from the Zone drop-down list box.

5. To change the security settings for the zone, click Zone Settings.

6. Drag the slider to set the security for that zone.

7. Click OK.

8. Click OK.

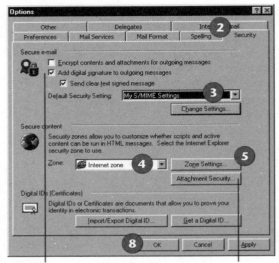

Select these check boxes to add default security settings to messages.

Click Attachment Security to define security settings for message attachments.

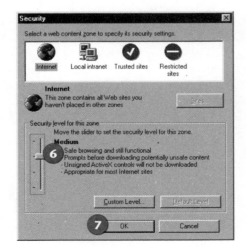

Using the Internet Connection Wizard

Internet Explorer's Internet Connection Wizard allows you to sign up for a new account with an Internet service provider and installs the account's settings for use with Outlook, Internet Explorer, and all other dial-up connections you make.

TIP

Reinstall account settings.
If you have an existing account with a service, and your account's settings have stopped working, you can often reinstall the account settings by running the Internet Connection Wizard and indicating you want to sign up for a new account with your existing service provider. When the service displays its Web page for signing up for a new account, see if there is an "I already have an existing account" option.

Sign Up for a New Internet Service

1 Click the Start button, choose Programs, choose Internet Explorer, and then click Internet Explorer Connection Wizard.

2 Click the first option button to sign up for a new service, and click Next. Outlook dials a toll-free number and displays a list of the Internet service providers in your area.

3 Select an Internet service provider (ISP) from the pane on the left to display information about it in the Provider Information pane.

4 Click Next to sign up for the selected service.

5 Fill out your personal information, and click Next.

6 Choose the specific access plan you want to have, and click Next.

7 Enter your credit card information, and click Next. Follow any instructions provided for setting up your new account, making sure to record your username and password.

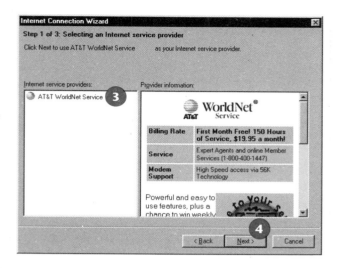

12

Adding and Removing Services from Your Profile

You can add and remove services you want to use with Outlook. For example, you can connect to another mailbox on your Exchange server, or you can add an Address Book, an Internet mail account, or a third-party mail service.

> **TIP**
>
> **Remove a service.** *To remove a service from your profile, select the service from the list box and click Remove.*

> **TIP**
>
> **Internet Only version.** *If you installed the Internet Only version of Outlook, your Tools menu doesn't have a Services command. To add another Internet mail account, choose Accounts from the Tools menu and click Add.*

Add a Service to Your Profile

1. Choose Services from the Tools menu.

2. Click Add.

3. Select the service you want to add to your profile from the drop-down list box.

4. Click OK. Depending on the service you choose, Outlook may ask you to define the service's properties.

Viewing Your Service Connection Properties

When you run the Internet Connection Wizard, it sets up the properties for your new account with your Internet service provider. You can view these properties or change them if necessary.

TIP

Leave a copy on the server. *To leave a copy of your e-mail messages on the server so you can retrieve them from a second location, click the Advanced tab and select the Leave A Copy Of Messages On Server check box.*

Display Your Service Properties

1. Choose Services from the Tools menu.

2. Select the service whose properties you want to view or edit from the drop-down list box.

3. Click Properties.

4. Use the tabs, buttons, and boxes Outlook displays for the service to make any changes to your account settings.

5. Click OK.

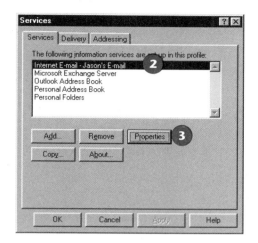

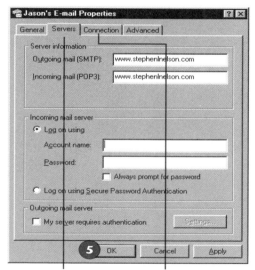

The Servers tab for an Internet mail service lists the mail and news servers.

The Connection tab for an Internet mail service lets you access the dial-up networking information.

12

Designating Profiles and Services

When you use Outlook, you can specify which profile you want to use. Your profile identifies you as the computer user and includes all the services you set up for that profile.

TIP

Enable offline access. *If your mail service supports it, select the Enable Offline Access check box to use Remote Mail or offline folders.*

Select a Profile and Services to Use with Outlook

1 Choose Options from the Tools menu.

2 Click the Mail Services tab.

3 Select the profile you want to use with Outlook from the drop-down list box, or click the Prompt For A Profile To Be Used option button if you want to be able to select a profile to use each time you start Outlook.

4 Select the services you want Outlook to check for new mail on when using the profile.

5 Click OK.

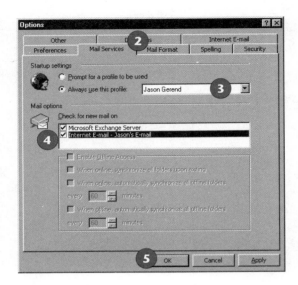

Adding a New Profile

If more than one person uses Outlook on your computer, you can set up additional profiles to identify the users. You can also set up more than one profile for yourself if you want to set up more than one Mailbox, Address Book, or set of services.

TIP

Sending mail stops working. *If sending mail in Outlook stops working, your profile may have become corrupted. Try adding a new profile, and then delete the old one.*

Add a New Profile to Your Computer

1 Click the Start button, choose Settings, and click Control Panel.

2 Double-click the Mail or the Mail And Fax icon.

3 Click Show Profiles.

4 Click Add.

5 In the Inbox Setup Wizard's first dialog box, select the services you want set up on this profile.

6 Click Next.

7 Use the wizard's next dialog boxes to describe the services you chose. Click Next to proceed to the next dialog box.

8 Click OK.

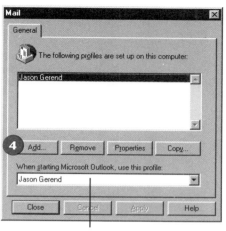

Use this drop-down list box to tell Outlook which profile to use.

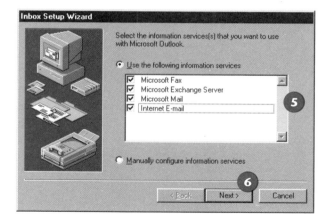

Index

electronic business cards, 43, 70

electronic mail. *See* e-mail

e-mail

adding message flags, 47

adding names to Address Book, 76

checking messages remotely, 26

collecting messages, 25

copying message text, 35

creating Address Book entries, 76

creating messages, 34

displaying messages, 27

formatting messages, 36–39

forwarding messages, 30

forwarding notes in messages, 145

inserting files into messages, 41

messages in HTML format, 28, 185

moving message text, 35

opening attachments, 31, 33

Outlook as e-mail client, 6–7, 23

printing attachments, 33

printing messages, 28

reading messages, 27

receiving attachments, 31

receiving messages, 24–25

replying to messages, 29

sending messages, 34, 50–51

sending messages to Personal Distribution Lists, 59, 79

setting defaults, 7, 185, 186–87

setting importance, 46

setting sensitivity, 46

specifying message format, 185

e-mail, *continued*

updating Address Book, 77

using Address Book, 78–79

viewing attachments, 31

viewing Inbox, 24

viewing Mail folders, 12, 13

viewing messages, 27

emptying Deleted Items folder, 21

encrypting messages, 45

events

annual, 103

vs. appointments, 102

creating event items, 102, 103

defined, 102

listing, 12, 95

recurring, 103

Exchange. *See* Microsoft Exchange

Expedia, 66–67

Express News. *See* Outlook Express News

faxes, sending and receiving, 23, 25, 34

files. *See also* attachments, e-mail

attaching to messages, 40

copying, 150

creating shortcuts to, 153

finding, 156

inserting in messages, 41

listing in My Computer, 148

moving, 153

opening in My Computer, 149

renaming, 150

saving folder items as, 157

searching for, 156

viewing properties, 149

filters, 170–71

finding. *See also* filters

Address Book names, 74

files, 156

folder items, 19

help information, 10

flagging e-mail messages, 47

floppy disks

copying, 151

formatting, 151

Folder Banner, 9

Folder list

displaying, 13, 148

illustrated, 9

vs. Outlook Bar, 174

folders. *See also* views

changing views, 162

cleaning up, 20

copying, 150

copying items between, 18

creating, 17, 152

creating shortcuts to, 17, 153

creating views, 172–73

customizing views, 166

Deleted Items folder, 20, 21

deleting items, 20

filtering items, 170–71

grouping items, 167

listing in Outlook Bar, 12, 13

moving, 153

moving items between, 18, 160

naming, 17, 152

new, 17, 152

overview, 5

printing item lists, 16

removing items, 165

renaming, 150

sharing on networks, 154

sorting items, 15, 168

switching between views, 162

undeleting items, 20

folders, *continued*

viewing mail in, 12, 13, 24

fonts, specifying, 36. *See also* text

formatting

e-mail messages, 36–39

floppy disks, 151

views, 169

forwarding

e-mail messages, 30

note items, 145

free/busy options, 110

frequently called phone numbers, 64

Global Address List, 71, 72. *See also* Address Book

grouping items, 167

groups

adding to Outlook Bar, 177

deleting, 177

illustrated, 9

renaming, 177

Help system, 10–11

hiding

folder items by filtering, 170–71

Journal timeline week numbers, 133

Outlook Bar, 174

status bar, 174

toolbars, 175

hours, task, 118

icons, Outlook Bar, 12, 13
importing Contacts list, 69
Inbox
  customizing, 186
  listing contents, 12, 24
  rules, 160–61
indenting text, 39
Information Viewer, defined, 9.
    See also views
installing Outlook, 6–7
Internet, scheduling meetings
    over, 7, 104
Internet Connection Wizard,
    193
Internet e-mail
  adding addresses to Contacts
    folder, 76
  customizing, 188–89
  finding names using
    directory services, 75
Internet Explorer
  mapping contacts using
    Expedia Maps, 66–67
  using Internet Connection
    Wizard, 193
  using NetMeeting, 106–7
Internet service providers, 195
italic text, 37
items. *See also* appointments;
    contacts; Journal;
    messages, e-mail; Notes
    folder; tasks
  archiving, 181
  assigning to categories, 164
  creating using AutoCreate, 18
  deleting, 20
  filtering, 170–71
  grouping, 167
  moving between folders, 18,
    160

items, *continued*
  opening from Journal, 130
  organizing, 160
  printing lists, 16
  recording, 124–27
  removing from categories,
    165
  retrieving after deleting, 20
  saving as files, 157
  searching for, 19
  sorting list, 15, 168
  undeleting, 20
  viewing, 14–15
  viewing in Preview Pane, 14

Journal
  categorizing entries, 164–65
  deleting entries, 134
  editing entries, 129
  entries as shortcuts to
    documents, 130
  moving entries, 134
  opening entries, 128
  overview, 123
  printing entries, 135
  recording activities, 124–27
  recording phone call time, 63
  removing entries, 134
  timeline for entries, 132–33
  viewing list of entries, 12
junk mail, 163

left-aligning paragraphs, 38
lists, creating, 38
lost items, 19

mail. *See* e-mail
mapping contacts, 66
meetings. *See also* NetMeeting
  attendee availability, 104
  attendee status, 104
  AutoPick feature, 104
  canceling, 105
  online, 105, 106–7
  planning, 104
  requesting, 105
  responding to requests, 105,
    111
  scheduling, 104–5
menu bar, 9
messages, e-mail
  adding message flags, 47
  adding signatures, 42–43
  adding voting buttons, 44
  checking remotely, 26
  collecting, 25
  color-coding, 161
  copying text, 35
  creating, 34
  delivery options, 48–49
  digitally signing, 45
  displaying, 27
  encrypting, 45
  expiration, 49
  and file shortcuts, 40
  formatting, 36–39
  forwarding, 30
  forwarding notes in, 145
  in HTML format, 28, 185
  inserting files, 41
  junk mail, 163
  moving text, 35
  opening attachments, 31, 33
  postponing delivery, 49
  printing, 28
  printing attachments, 33

messages, e-mail, *continued*
  reading, 27
  receiving, 24–25
  receiving attachments, 31
  replying to, 29
  security options, 192
  sending, 34, 50–51
  sending to Personal Distribu-
    tion Lists, 59, 79
  setting defaults, 7, 185, 186–
    87
  setting importance, 46
  setting sensitivity, 46
  specifying format, 185
  tracking, 48
  using Address Book to send,
    78–79
  viewing, 27
  viewing attachments, 31
  viewing lists in Mail folders,
    12, 13, 24
  and viruses, 32
messages, newsgroup
  downloading, 88–89
  posting, 92
  reading, 90
  saving attachments, 91
  viewing, 86
Microsoft Exchange
  Global Address List, 71, 72
  Personal Address Book, 71,
    72
  receiving e-mail, 25
  tracking e-mail, 48
Microsoft Expedia, 66–67
Microsoft NetMeeting, 106–7
Microsoft Office
  creating new documents, 152
  opening documents from
    Journal, 130
  recording documents, 124,
    127

phone numbers
adding to contact information, 54, 55
adding to Speed Dialing list,
64
dialing, 62–63
frequently called, 64
redialing, 65
removing from Speed Dialing
list, 65
previewing printing, 16, 60
Preview pane, 9, 14, 27, 33, 182
printing
appointment details, 101
calendars, 101
contact items, 60–61
e-mail attachments, 33
e-mail messages, 28
folder item lists, 16
Journal entries, 135
Microsoft Expedia maps, 67
note items, 144
previewing before printing,
16, 60
using Print button vs. Print
command, 16, 28
privacy. *See also* security
making appointments
private, 96
making tasks private, 114
profiles
adding services, 194
creating, 197
designating, 196
removing services, 194
properties
Address Book, 81
Internet service providers,
195
viewing file properties, 149

R

reading messages, 27
receiving
e-mail attachments, 31
e-mail messages, 24–25
recording activities
automatically, 124–25
manually, 126–27
recording Microsoft Office
documents, 124, 127
recurring items
appointments, 100, 103
events, 103
tasks, 115
Recycle Bin, 21
redialing phone numbers, 65
reminders
for appointments, 98–99
setting defaults, 99, 110, 184
for tasks, 121
Remote Mail, 26
renaming
Address Book, 81
files, 150
folders, 150
groups, 177
tasks, 117
replying to e-mail messages, 29
requests
meeting, 105, 111
task, 119
rescheduling appointments, 97
resizing note windows, 142
Rich Text Format, 144
right-aligning paragraphs, 38
rules, Inbox, 160–61

S

saving
e-mail attachments, 32
folder items as files, 157
Schedule+ contact lists,
importing, 69
scheduling meetings, 104–5
searching. *See also* filters
for Address Book names, 74
for files, 156
for folder items, 19
for help information, 10
security
making appointments
private, 96
making tasks private, 114
and Personal Distribution
Lists, 59
setting options, 192
sending
e-mail messages, 34, 50–51
Personal Distribution List
messages, 59, 79
Sent Items folder, 13
sharing folders on networks,
154. *See also* assigning
tasks; meetings
shortcuts
adding to Outlook Bar, 176,
177
creating, 17, 153
Journal entries as, 130
signatures
adding to messages, 43
creating, 42
types of files, 42
sizing note windows, 142

sorting
Address Book names, 80
contacts, 54
items in views, 15, 168
task list, 116
sound files, 98, 184
speed dialing, 64–65
spelling checker, setting
defaults, 191
status bar, 174
switching between views, 162

task list. *See also* TaskPad
adding tasks, 114–15
changing task due dates, 117
changing task options, 121
changing view, 122
creating, 114–15
customizing, 121
deleting tasks, 114
list of task view options, 122
marking tasks completed,
117
monitoring task progress,
118, 120
opening task items, 116
prioritizing tasks, 114
recurring tasks, 115
renaming tasks, 117
sending task status information to others, 120
setting tracking default, 119
sorting tasks by due date, 116
start and end dates, 114, 115
updating task status, 118
viewing, 122
viewing from Outlook Bar, 12

The manuscript for this book was prepared and submitted to Microsoft Press in electronic form. Text files were prepared using Microsoft Word 97. Pages were composed by Stephen L. Nelson, Inc., using PageMaker for Windows, with text in Stone Sans and display type in Stone Serif and Stone Serif Semibold. Composed pages were delivered to the printer as electronic prepress files.

Cover Designer

Tim Girvin Design

Graphic Layout

Stefan Knorr

Indexer

Julie Kawabata

Keep fast answers
in your pocket!

MICROSOFT POCKET GUIDES are portable, reliable references to Microsoft Office 2000 applications, ideal for the frequent traveler or anyone seeking quick answers about each application's tools, terms, and techniques. To find everything you need to know to put Office 2000 to work today, trust MICROSOFT POCKET GUIDES—learning solutions, made by Microsoft.

- MICROSOFT® POCKET GUIDE TO MICROSOFT EXCEL 2000
- MICROSOFT POCKET GUIDE TO MICROSOFT WORD 2000
- MICROSOFT POCKET GUIDE TO MICROSOFT ACCESS 2000
- MICROSOFT POCKET GUIDE TO MICROSOFT POWERPOINT® 2000
- MICROSOFT POCKET GUIDE TO MICROSOFT OUTLOOK™ 2000
- MICROSOFT POCKET GUIDE TO MICROSOFT INTERNET EXPLORER 5

mspress.microsoft.com

Master
Microsoft® Office 2000
in a hurry!

Microsoft Press Quick Course® books offer you streamlined instruction in the form of no-nonsense, to-the-point tutorials and learning exercises. The core of each book is a logical sequence of straightforward, easy-to-follow instructions for building useful business skills—the same skills that you use on the job.

- QUICK COURSE® IN MICROSOFT® EXCEL 2000
- QUICK COURSE IN MICROSOFT ACCESS 2000
- QUICK COURSE IN MICROSOFT OFFICE 2000
- QUICK COURSE IN MICROSOFT POWERPOINT® 2000
- QUICK COURSEIN MICROSOFT WORD 2000
- QUICK COURSEIN MICROSOFT FRONTPAGE® 2000
- QUICK COURSEIN MICROSOFT INTERNET EXPLORER 5
- QUICK COURSE IN MICROSOFT PUBLISHER 2000
- QUICK COURSE IN MICROSOFT OUTLOOK® 2000

mspress.microsoft.com

Stay in the *running* for maximum productivity.

These are *the* answer books for business users of Microsoft® Office 2000. They are packed with everything from quick, clear instructions for new users to comprehensive answers for power users—the authoritative reference to keep by your computer and use every day. THE RUNNING SERIES—learning solutions made by Microsoft.

- RUNNING MICROSOFT EXCEL 2000
- RUNNING MICROSOFT OFFICE 2000 PREMIUM
- RUNNING MICROSOFT OFFICE 2000 PROFESSIONAL
- RUNNING MICROSOFT OFFICE 2000 SMALL BUSINESS EDITION
- RUNNING MICROSOFT WORD 2000
- RUNNING MICROSOFT POWERPOINT® 2000
- RUNNING MICROSOFT ACCESS 2000
- RUNNING MICROSOFT INTERNET EXPLORER 5.0
- RUNNING MICROSOFT FRONTPAGE®
- RUNNING MICROSOFT OUTLOOK® 2000

mspress.microsoft.com

Step up!

STEP BY STEP books provide quick and easy self-training—to help you learn to use the powerful word processing, spreadsheet, database, presentation, communication, and Internet components of Microsoft Office 2000—both individually and together. The easy-to-follow lessons present clear objectives and real-world business examples, with numerous screen shots and illustrations. Put Office 2000 to work today, with STEP BY STEP learning solutions, made by Microsoft.

- MICROSOFT® OFFICE PROFESSONAL 8-IN-1 STEP BY STEP
- MICROSOFT WORD 2000 STEP BY STEP
- MICROSOFT EXCEL 2000 STEP BY STEP
- MICROSOFT POWERPOINT® 2000 STEP BY STEP
- MICROSOFT INTERNET EXPLORER 5 STEP BY STEP
- MICROSOFT PUBLISHER 2000 STEP BY STEP
- MICROSOFT ACCESS 2000 STEP BY STEP
- MICROSOFT FRONTPAGE 2000 STEP BY STEP
- MICROSOFT OUTLOOK 2000 STEP BY STEP

mspress.microsoft.com

Register Today!

Return this
Microsoft® Outlook™ 2000 At a Glance
registration card today

Microsoft® Press
mspress.microsoft.com

OWNER REGISTRATION CARD   1-57231-948-8

Microsoft® Outlook™ 2000 At a Glance

FIRST NAME   MIDDLE INITIAL   LAST NAME

INSTITUTION OR COMPANY NAME

ADDRESS

CITY   STATE   ZIP

                                                  ( )
E-MAIL ADDRESS   PHONE NUMBER

U.S. and Canada addresses only. Fill in information above and mail postage-free.
Please mail only the bottom half of this page.

For information about Microsoft Press®
products, visit our Web site at
mspress.microsoft.com

Microsoft·Press